More Praise for *When the Headline Is You*

"*When the Headline Is You* is the best book I've read on how to ensure every press interaction results in fair and balanced coverage for you and your company."
—Greg Pruett, senior vice president, Corporate Affairs, PG&E Corporation

"After more than 30 years as a journalist and then a communications practitioner, everything in *When the Headline Is You* rings true to me. Jeff Ansell's strategies work."
—Roy Thomas, continuing education instructor in Journalism, Ryerson University

"Each page has stories and each story has lessons. It is not a book to read only once. Soon your copy of *When the Headline Is You* will be just as dog-eared as mine and will always be a part of your briefing binders."
—Jean-Michel Halfon, president and general manager, Emerging Markets Business Unit, Pfizer

"*When the Headline Is You* is a must-read for anyone in front of or behind the news camera."
—Ian Mitroff, crisis management expert and university professor

"Jeff Ansell was one of the most focused, energetic, and unrelenting reporters I've ever known. He's always known how to dig into a story and tell it well."
—Thalia Assuras, former *CBS News* anchor

When the Headline Is You

When the Headline Is You

An Insider's Guide to Handling the Media

Jeff Ansell with Jeffrey Leeson

JOSSEY-BASS
A Wiley Imprint
www.josseybass.com

Published by Jossey-Bass
A Wiley Imprint
989 Market Street, San Francisco, CA 94103-1741—www.josseybass.com

Jossey-Bass books and products are available through most bookstores. To contact Jossey-Bass directly call our Customer Care Department within the U.S. at 800-956-7739, outside the U.S. at 317-572-3986, or fax 317-572-4002.

Jossey-Bass also publishes its books in a variety of electronic formats. Some content that appears in print may not be available in electronic books.

Library of Congress Cataloging-in-Publication Data

Ansell, Jeff, 1955-
    When the headline is you : an insider's guide to handling the media / Jeff Ansell with Jeffrey Leeson.
        p. cm. — (J-B international association of business communicators ; 10)
    Includes bibliographical references and index.
    ISBN 978-0-470-54394-8 (hardback)
    1. Public relations.   2. Publicity.   3. Interviewing in mass media.   I. Leeson, Jeffrey, 1969-
II. Title.
    HM1221.A57 2010
    659.2—dc22

                                                                                    2010024702

Printed in the United States of America
FIRST EDITION
HB Printing   10 9 8 7 6 5 4 3 2 1

Contents

For my mother and father

Foreword

During my two decades in corporate communications, I have not seen the financial and business community facing as skeptical a public as we are today. The world of news and information is fast-moving—no sooner done than said, in fact. As the executive who heads global external and internal communications and public relations activities for the Ford Motor Company, I see a press corps more probing than ever. Jeff Ansell's new book *When the Headline Is You* is a timely and invaluable must-read not only for public relations and communications professionals but for anyone in business, government, or the nonprofit sector dealing with a roused public and emboldened media—both "old" and "new."

No one argues more forcefully than Jeff Ansell that the skills required to cope with the current environment often are subtle and have a great deal to do with appropriate language—those make-or-break words and phrases that are essential. For most people, these skills do not come naturally. They have to be taught, learned, and practiced, which is why this instructive volume is so on-target. Unlike some who offer such counsel, Jeff approaches the task from both sides of the divide, having racked up impressive credentials as a journalist before launching a notably successful career as a public relations practitioner and business educator.

When the Headline Is You has unique power and value thanks to the numerous real-life examples and case histories literally torn from today's headlines. Jeff frequently and effectively cites them to illustrate how the wrong or right responses can make a critical, game-changing difference. These insights are what make this a how-to book that provides virtually everything a communicator needs to know from someone who really knows.

Ray Day
Vice President, Communications
Ford Motor Company

Introduction

Answering questions from reporters is risky business. Though a media interview may feel like a straightforward conversation, it actually represents a contrived and manipulative dynamic. Knowing how to talk to reporters is like learning a new language, a language that bears little if any resemblance to everyday conversation. It is a mistake for anyone to believe otherwise. It may seem as if speaking the truth should be enough to build credibility and trust, but that's rarely the case. Exposing oneself to media scrutiny requires more than simple candor. It requires knowledge, training, and a keen understanding of how reporters write the news.

In my nearly forty years of experience, I have yet to meet anyone for whom media skills come naturally. Answering tough questions from reporters is even difficult for reporters themselves. You would think being skilled in asking questions would provide insight into how best to answer them. I discovered otherwise, however, in a training session for famed Watergate journalist Carl Bernstein. In the training, my first question to Carl was whether he had a troubled relationship with his Watergate partner Bob Woodward. To my surprise, Carl put his foot in his mouth so deeply it came out the other end. I learned something important that day. Anyone can ask questions. The real skill is in answering them.

It should be of little surprise, then, that many executives, government leaders, and spokespeople are reluctant to engage the news media. Their concern is justified. People who talk to the media are only as good as their worst quote. Though someone answering a reporter's questions may strike all the right notes for the majority of the interview, it takes only a single miscue to trigger disaster. One misstatement to a reporter can destroy long-held goodwill or cause a company's share price to plummet. As legendary investor Warren Buffet said, "It takes twenty years to build a reputation and five minutes to ruin it."[1]

Historically, public relations professionals and media trainers have told clients to ignore questions they don't like and instead repeat scripted messages. The end result is that many people who talk to reporters come across as evasive and unresponsive. This approach to communicating—or rather the lack of it—has led to record levels of skepticism and distrust among the general public. To be better media communicators, newsmakers and spokespeople must learn how to answer confrontational questions with integrity while still limiting their exposure to the sensationalism of today's media environment. Using a values-based approach, *When the Headline Is You* provides a framework for addressing problematic issues in an open, forthright manner that eliminates both the possibility of misinterpretation and the risk of being taken out of context.

Offering strategies for navigating all types of media encounters, *When the Headline Is You* is intended to help everyone who interacts with journalists or reporters, including executives, spokespeople, PR representatives, and corporate communication professionals. The book will be equally helpful to the message makers behind the scenes: the public relations practitioners and communication consultants tasked with preparing media messages for challenging, newsworthy situations. In addition, academics and students in communication and journalism will find many of the real-world scenarios useful in developing a deeper understanding of how the media operates and building the core skills necessary to become persuasive communicators.

In providing a framework for creating meaningful messages, *When the Headline Is You* focuses on key principles and proven strategies for success in today's media-saturated world. I've organized these principles and strategies into clearly defined steps that mirror the process of preparing for a media encounter. This structure offers readers both the fundamental knowledge and the practical tools necessary to manage image and reputation even under the most stressful circumstances.

I start in Chapter One by providing an overview of how news is made, reported, and interpreted. In Chapter Two, readers will learn how to manage the initial encounter with a journalist, avoid common interview traps, and align organizational image with positive values. Chapter Three explains the key principles for building trust and provides a simple yet powerful formula for crafting bad news messages. In Chapter Four, I examine many different types of media messages and discuss a template for creating a comprehensive range of compelling responses and statements. Chapter Five follows with an in-depth discussion of successful public speaking techniques that will help readers optimize message delivery. Chapter Six examines difficult situations like surprise encounters and provides step-by-step strategies for effectively managing these situations. Finally, in Chapter Seven, I present specific techniques for answering twenty of the most potentially damaging questions that spokespeople commonly encounter.

Throughout the book, I've incorporated a number of special features and practical tools, including:

- A complete Media Messaging Toolkit with reproducible templates and worksheets
- Actual news stories and interview transcripts that bring concepts to life and illustrate essential media communication lessons
- Sidebars that add context to salient ideas and provide additional practical strategies
- Proven public speaking tips and a six-step message-delivery exercise that's guaranteed to improve your presentation skills

- A recurring, illustrative example that depicts the entire media messaging process and clearly demonstrates implementation techniques
- Chapter-ending "Talking Points" to help you review and reference critical concepts

When the Headline Is You is designed so you can easily navigate each chapter and locate specific topics and practical information. This means you can jump from chapter to chapter and pull out what you need, when you need it. But there's also an advantage to reading the chapters in order. The chapters are clearly linked and the techniques presented build on each other to facilitate your skill development.

No matter how you choose to use the book, my hope is that everyone who picks it up discovers valuable strategies and messaging formulae to use in communicating with reporters. Whether delivering good news, not-so-good news, or dealing with a full-blown media crisis, *When the Headline Is You* provides a process for crafting responsive messages that present your organization in a proactive, positive manner.

When the Headline Is You

1

WHAT IS NEWS?

"News is what I say it is."
—*David Brinkley, former network anchor*

Julius Caesar created the world's first newspaper in the year 59 BC. The *Acta Diurna*, or *Daily Doings*, was posted on walls across Rome. Its purpose was to keep the Roman senate under scrutiny. We've gone from walls to Web logs, but reporters still hold people accountable, only now they do it through TV, magazines, newspapers, satellite radio, and the Internet. Today, anyone anywhere can generate news and share information. This convenience comes at a price, however. Research on the run only gets it right some of the time, and truth and perspective become casualties of reporting. "The newspaper that drops on your doorstep is a partial, hasty, incomplete, inevitably somewhat flawed, and inaccurate rendering of some of the things we heard about in the past twenty-four hours," wrote Pulitzer Prize–winning reporter David Broder.[1] Avoiding becoming a victim of these discrepancies and inconsistencies begins with a clear understanding of how the press operates. This chapter will give you a peek behind the media curtain to see how news is made, reported, and ultimately interpreted.

If It Bleeds, It Leads

Chief executives, politicians, and celebrities have long complained of media callousness and sensationalism. Musician Don

Henley of the Eagles has such contempt for reporters that he wrote "Dirty Laundry," a song about news anchors who worry more about their looks than they do about the news or its repercussions. "We got the bubble-headed bleach blond who comes on at five," Henley sings. "She can tell you 'bout the plane crash with a gleam in her eye."[2]

Based on my personal experience, Henley was not far off the mark. I vividly recall one particularly disturbing instance. It was a slow news day and the producer of the six o'clock news was upset because we did not have a good lead story to open the broadcast. All we had as a possible lead story was a stabbing that had taken place. Then, a half hour before we went on air, the assignment editor came on the loudspeaker in the newsroom and announced that there was good news—the stabbing victim had died. My colleagues in the newsroom erupted into a cheer. Now they had a lead story for the six o'clock news. That was the day I left journalism.

Since that time, the news business has evolved dramatically. Names and faces have changed, papers have come and gone, and the world of media has become fractured, with the Web altering what and who make up the news media. Still, what constitutes news and how news stories are shaped has remained surprisingly consistent since the days of Caesar's first newspaper.

News Is . . .

The process of determining what makes news is not very sophisticated. Generally, news is whatever will help sell papers and ad space. Often, this means news is anything that shocks, titillates, or angers readers or viewers. Certainly, there is plenty of scandal and gossip in the media to distract or entice the masses these days. But even if there was a shortage of news to report, journalists would still need to find news somewhere. Following are the fundamental "building blocks" used to identify, structure, and develop news stories.

Conflict.   The reporter's quest is for conflict, not solutions. Solutions interfere with conflict, and conflict is how reporters earn a living. News stories that feature conflict are more compelling and easy to replicate. "Our training, the news value we inculcate, the feedback we get from our editors, all encourage us to look for trouble, for failure, for scandal, above all for conflict," writes syndicated columnist William Raspberry.[3]

Good News Is Still News

With a faltering economy and ongoing global conflict, it's sometimes easy to forget that news is also about good news: A lost child found unharmed or a teacher who makes a difference. A species saved from extinction or a possible cure for cancer. These types of good deeds and civic-minded or humanitarian acts constitute news as much as the most recent murder, political gaffe, or celebrity rumor. Take, for example, the plight of US Airways flight 1549. With both engines disabled by a flock of geese, Captain Chesley "Sully" Sullenberger made a perfect emergency landing in the Hudson River, saving 155 lives. Or consider Dendreon Corporation, a small biotech company that overcame intense financial pressures and regulatory hurdles to pioneer a new, more effective way to treat prostate cancer, one of the world's deadliest diseases. These types of stories may not get as many headlines or column inches as the latest serial killer or an aging celebrity's fertility treatments, but virtue and heroism will always play a role in determining the news.

Good Versus Evil.   The good-versus-evil model is a boiler-plate for writing and reporting the news. This is no surprise, considering that good versus evil is a universal theme in storytelling and has been since the beginning of language. The Bible has stories about good versus evil, such as Cain and Abel or Moses and the Pharaoh. Books and movies are built on good-versus-evil stories. And much like stories about conflict, news reports centering on good versus evil are easy to write.

Winners and Losers. From the sports section to the opinion page, news is about keeping score. Who won the game, who lost the debate. Who had the best box office and whose stock cratered after disappointing earnings. In the world of reporting, every situation represents "triumph or disaster," according to former British Prime Minister Tony Blair. Every "problem is a crisis and a setback is a policy in tatters," he added.[4]

Bad Decisions. Bad decisions are an inevitable part of life. We all make them. Most are forgotten, but sometimes a really bad decision can land you on the front page. Take the case of Andrew Speaker. Even though he was diagnosed with a contagious drug-resistant strain of tuberculosis, he boarded an international flight, exposing others to risk. "In hindsight, maybe it wasn't the best decision," Speaker said in a *Good Morning America* interview with Diane Sawyer.

Irony. There are numerous types and dozens of definitions of irony. Most people think of it as an incongruity between expectations and results. It has also come to signify unfortunate and surprising coincidences. Take the story of the Florida woman pulled over for speeding and being drunk. Not a particularly remarkable story, right? But what was ironic—and what made it news—is that her job at the time was to teach police how to enforce drunk-driving laws.

Rumors. Regardless of how ridiculous they may be, rumors are certain to attract attention from the press. As any high schooler can tell you, many rumors take on a life of their own. For instance, word circulated in the Toronto suburb of Brampton that a new government program was offering poor people $10,000 to leave the city and move to Brampton. As silly as it sounds, even the *Toronto Star* reported on the mythical "program."

The Unusual or Absurd. People have always been fascinated by the odd, unusual, and unlikely. "Puppy Shoots Florida Man," read the September 21, 2004, Associated Press headline for a story about Trigger, a mixed shepherd, who put his paw on the trigger of a gun and shot his owner in the arm. The shooting took place after the owner killed three of Trigger's littermates. Much else happened in the world that day, yet it was the Trigger story that was featured on front pages everywhere. Was it because people love animals? Of course. But face it, stories about dogs shooting their owners don't come along every day.

Maggie and the Stones

For a novice journalist learning how to recognize news, there is no substitute for on-the-job experience. However, naiveté can lead to lost opportunity. Working in the newsroom one evening in the late 1970s, I received an anonymous phone tip that Maggie Trudeau, then-wife of Canadian Prime Minister Pierre Trudeau, was partying with the Rolling Stones at the El Mocambo Club in Toronto. To my young mind, the idea that the wife of the prime minister would pal around with the Rolling Stones seemed ridiculous. Foolishly, I failed to investigate.

The next day, a local newspaper featured front-page photos of Maggie dancing and partying you know where, with you know whom. The story became news all over the world. Had I sensed the newsworthiness of the tip and followed up, I could have been the one to discover that Maggie invited the Stones back to her room to "drink, play dice, smoke a little hash," as she later revealed. The Maggie Trudeau/Rolling Stones story was certainly not worthy of a Pulitzer, but it was unusual. That day I learned an important lesson as a reporter: sometimes the most important factor in recognizing what makes news is to accept a situation or fact that, at first blush, may seem absurd.

Offensive Comments.   Reporters covet offensive comments made by famous people. In 2006, Israeli President Moshe Katsav was accused of raping ten female staff members. Soon after, Russian President Vladimir Putin and Israeli Prime Minister Ehud Olmert met in Moscow for a diplomatic summit. When the issue of Katsav was raised during a news conference, Putin joked, "I would never have expected this from him. He surprised us all. We all envy him." As inappropriate as that comment was, it is overshadowed by what a former client of mine told a business reporter before I was brought in to help. The client, chairman of a high-tech company, was responding to an allegation that a senior executive raped a staff member. "I don't believe it—she's not even good-looking," he said.

Uninformed Politicians.   Politicians who do not have answers to simple questions are sure to find themselves featured on CNN, MSNBC, and FOX News. U.S. Senate candidate Pete Coors was caught unprepared when his opponent Bob Schaeffer questioned him about Canadian Prime Minister Paul Martin's position on the Canadian beef ban. "I don't know Paul Martin's whole position on this issue," said Coors, adding, "I'm not sure I know who Paul Martin is." Candidate Schaeffer shot back, "What I'm disappointed and shocked about is that you don't know who Paul Martin is. Paul Martin is the prime minister of Canada, our largest trade partner and closest friend and ally to the north."

Failed Jokes.   Sometimes jokes just don't come across correctly. Senator John Kerry decided not to run for president in 2008 after being vilified for mangling a joke he told to college students in Pasadena, California. "Education, if you make the most of it, you study hard, you do your homework, and you make an effort to be smart, you can do well. If you don't, you get stuck in Iraq," said Kerry. Most who heard the joke thought Kerry called U.S. soldiers uneducated. Kerry said that he actually meant to say, ". . . you end up getting stuck in a war in Iraq. Just ask President Bush."

While news isn't always about drunk police instructors or dogs that shoot people, it almost always is a story that has been reduced to its most dramatic or sensationalized elements. Decisions about what makes the news—or for that matter, what doesn't make the news—are in the hands of people who use very basic criteria, as well as their personal reference points, to determine which stories, situations, or issues are worthy of reporting. In trying to make this determination, one of the most important criteria is whether a story has obvious, though compelling, "characters."

Reporters Cast Characters

Ask most journalists how they see news and their response will likely be about the pursuit of truth. To pursue truth is indeed a noble path. To get to their truth, journalists, news producers, and editors cast characters and build stories around them—stories that involve controversy, conflict, and emotion. The problem, of course, is in the ambiguity of interpreting truth itself. As revealed in Brinkley's quote at the top of this chapter about news being what he says it is, one person's terrorist is another person's freedom fighter. But who gets to decide which player is the terrorist and which is the freedom fighter?

Reporters, along with editors and producers, decide who plays the hero or villain in a story. Like Steven Spielberg, they hand out roles for tonight's evening news and tomorrow morning's newspaper. Starring roles are reserved for the protagonist and the antagonist, the hero and the villain. Supporting roles are available for the victim, witness, survivor, expert, and goat—or as I like to call that character, the village idiot. Usually, it is the village idiot who caused the problem in the first place. On occasion, the village idiot also stars as the villain.

A front-page headline in the July 28, 2005 edition of Canada's *Globe and Mail* newspaper read, "A Landlord, an Eviction, and a Dying Man's Last Wish." The story was about a twenty-nine-year-old terminal cancer patient being evicted because he owed his landlord $1,600. Asked whether she had sympathy for the sick tenant, the landlord snapped, "What am I, his mother? Why do I have to support him?" At first glance, the roles are clear. The terminal patient is cast as both the good guy and the victim, while the landlord is cast as the villain. But how do we know that was indeed the case? It's possible that the patient was a tenant from hell and that the landlord had carried him for as long as she possibly could.

In truth, personal bias determines who gets cast in which roles. Journalists are not comfortable discussing personal bias. The role of the journalist, they believe, is simply to report the truth. Never having given it much thought during my reporting days, I suppose that my personal biases led me to become an investigative reporter. My biases were triggered by resentment I felt as a youngster over how my father was callously laid off by uncaring factory owners. Becoming a journalist allowed me to meet, challenge, and hold accountable people I perceived (rightly or wrongly) as high and mighty. To me, working-class characters were heroes, while politicians, employers, and landlords were among those cast as the villain.

On occasion, the media creates heroes only to turn them into goats. In seeking the GOP nomination in 2008, Senator John McCain's campaign was given up for dead, when suddenly it was resurrected and McCain became a darling of the media. Then, as he was about to secure the Republican nomination, a *New York Times* story by Elizabeth Bumiller suggested that McCain had an inappropriate relationship with a female lobbyist thirty years his junior. There was no proof of impropriety offered in the story, only nameless sources serving up gossip and innuendo. Though no fan of McCain, conservative commentator Rush Limbaugh said, "If you let the media make you, you are subjecting yourself to the media being able to destroy you." Is it any wonder people are gun shy of reporters?

In Defense of Reporters

The stress faced by reporters is very real. Editors and producers don't care about the great story the journalist wrote yesterday; what matters is the story she writes today.

This pressure on reporters is more intense than ever, according to Canadian Press reporter Chinta Puxley, who writes for newspapers, posts on the Web, files audio stories, and also carries a video camera. Deadlines are constant, says Puxley. "Once you meet one deadline for an audio window, you're working to the next deadline for the wire, for the website filing video. It's tremendously busy." Puxley adds that the Web and the use of video has created greater urgency in getting the news out. "People are getting their news in totally different ways. You can't work to the same type of deadline that people are used to. The pace of journalism has skyrocketed and it changes the way reporters are doing their job. A lot of reporters have to adjust to putting their story out on the Web a little earlier and then writing a totally different story for the next day's paper."

A "paint-by-numbers" approach to news reporting facilitates the continual grinding out of news, making it simpler for journalists to write stories quickly. Few journalists would admit as much, however, because the implication would be that they prejudge the outcome of their reports and the people they interview before writing the story. By using an established formula and relying on archetypes to quickly write news stories, journalists are better able to cope with the constant pressure created by attempting to write history in a hurry.

Social Media Raises the Stakes

The term *social media* refers to the use of technology to facilitate interaction and the sharing of information, opinions, and experiences. Forms of social media include blogs, which are websites that offer posts where readers can provide comment; forums, where a wide number of users discuss topics online; and social networks like Facebook and Twitter, the free microblogging service that lets users connect with each other using 140 characters or less. MySpace, Technorati, digg.com, and a growing list of other social media communication tools round out the options.

Social media represents much more than tools to entertain oneself or allow old friends to catch up. It offers reporters, companies, governments, and newsmakers powerful ways to communicate. Social media in general and blogs in particular have become an important resource for journalists. According to *PR Week Magazine*, in the course of researching a story, 29 percent of reporters look to general blogs, 25 percent use company blogs, and 24 percent use social networks.[5]

In addition, social networks are updated 24/7. Former *Time Magazine* employee Erick Schonfeld, who writes for TechCrunch, believes this immediacy provides a new way of getting at the truth. Sometimes, says Schonfeld, he'll run a story online before all the facts are in, just to see what the story turns up. "More often than not, putting up partial information is what leads us to the truth—a source contacts us with more details or adds them directly into comments."[6] But the use of social media as a means to disseminate information and propagate news is not limited to professional journalists. Witness the explosive growth of "citizen journalists"—people who report news for free and share it with the world online.

A decade ago, corporations were giddy with excitement about going online, reaching around the world, and communicating with anyone who would pay attention. Today, companies no longer control what is being said on the Web. Similarly, traditional journalists who write for print and broadcast media are not the only purveyors of information and news. "We are all newsmen now," said pioneer blogger Matt Drudge.[7]

The general public, customers, critics, and your competitors are now among those online discussing your company. According to *The Blog Herald*, a monitor of the blogosphere, a new blog is created every second of every day. In the ten minutes it takes to set up a free account at Blogger or other such sites, anyone with a computer and Internet connection can instantly become a blog publisher, reporter, saboteur, or critic. In many online venues, the balance of power has shifted from corporations and media conglomerates to the average person.

Just think, three years after Twitter's launch in 2006, it was estimated that seven million people were tweeting regularly and sharing information that runs from the mundane to the meaningful. In Korea, more than seventy thousand citizens contribute to *OhmyNews*, which is run by former investigative journalist Yeon Ho Oh. The site receives, on average, two and a half million page views a day. The BBC and *Time Magazine* have described this model for citizen journalism as the future of the media industry. NowPublic.com, a North American citizen journalism company based in Vancouver and ranked by *Time Magazine* as one of the Top 50 Best Sites of 2007, has tens of thousands of citizen journalists all over the world—five thousand in Washington, D.C., alone.

Does this mean that people who tweet, blog, and contribute to online forums will replace trained journalists? Not all are convinced of blogger bona fides. Tom McPhail, professor of journalism at the University of Missouri, has called bloggers "pretend journalists" who "thrive on rumor and innuendo."[8] Political journalist Glenn Greenwald is more generous in his perspective. "There are alternative voices now," said Greenwald. "The Internet enables people to construct their own platforms and to attract like-minded people, so that now there are gathering places of hundreds of thousands, if not more, citizens who are just as angry, just as dissatisfied."[9]

Regardless of one's perspective on the impact of bloggers, a few points are clear: social media is anything but a passing fad;

bloggers and other social media proponents will constantly place pressure on news companies to report the news faster and more transparently; and despite the technologies people use to get their news now and in the future, investigative journalism is here to stay. "It doesn't matter if it's a five thousand word story in a newspaper, a tweet, or a blog," said John Stackhouse, editor-in-chief of the *Globe and Mail.* "The basic challenges are the same: finding out information that matters to people."[10]

Much Can Go Wrong

With an ever-expanding number of professional reporters, citizen journalists, and bloggers vying to break the next big story, executives and spokespeople must take potential threats to their organization's reputation more seriously. According to crisis management expert Ian Mitroff, author of *Why Some Companies Emerge Stronger and Better from a Crisis,* "Every organization is virtually guaranteed to experience at least one major crisis."[11] A look at the daily papers appears to confirm Mitroff's premise. On one day alone, the *Wall Street Journal* featured the following headlines:

- "Bristol Myers Ex Officials are Indicted"
- "KPMG Faces Criminal Cases on Tax Shelters"
- "Tribune Ex Aides Are Arrested Over False Circulation Scams"
- "Bluetooth Gear May Be Open to Snooping"
- "Death on Disney Ride Remains a Mystery"
- "Marin Capital Closes up Shop amid Losses"[12]

Interestingly, however, a survey done by PR firm Weber Shandwick found that nearly half of CEOs questioned were slightly or not concerned at all about threats to their reputation.[13] To some, a good reputation is nice if you have one, but bottom-line results are what count. Unfortunately, this attitude ignores a significant body of research and numerous metrics that measure the value of a company's reputation through parameters like market share, price premium, revenue generation, transaction value, lifetime value of brand, and brand growth. The simplest of these metrics is derived by taking the current market capitalization of a company and deducting the tangible assets and accounts receivable to determine the value of its reputation. Another simple method is to compare the company's products to similar name-brand products or competing generics. Are consumers willing to pay a price premium for the name on the label? But despite these metrics that measure image and public perception in actual dollar terms, reputation is still dismissed as an intangible that has little effect on current and future performance.

Factors That Can Significantly Damage Reputation

What do business executives believe are the potential crises that could have the greatest potential to damage their company's reputation? Here's what a survey by PR firm Weber Shandwick revealed:[14]

Issue	Percent of Business Executives
Financial irregularities	72
Unethical behavior	68
Executive misconduct	64
Security breaches such as loss of confidential information	62
Environmental violations	60
Product recall based on health and safety issues	60
Regulatory noncompliance	59
Factory breakdowns or explosions resulting in injuries	59
Labor strikes or unrest	40
Ongoing protests by special interest groups or NGOs	38

Issue	Percent of Business Executives
Risky supply chain partners	38
Support of unpopular public policy position	38
Public controversies over high CEO compensation	36
Online attacks or rumors	25
Top executive departures	17

Consider the case of Union Carbide. In 1984, a Union Carbide–owned pesticide plant in Bhopal, India, released a toxic cloud that killed thirty-eight hundred people and disabled eleven thousand more. Though they launched an aggressive media campaign, Union Carbide never took responsibility for the accident. Instead, it claimed the disaster was caused by an unknown and unidentified disgruntled employee. Critics, however, pointed to previous accidents at the facility and asserted the tragedy was a result of poor maintenance and lax safety measures. Because of the controversy surrounding culpability, the disaster became a continual headline for decades. Civil and criminal litigation persist even now, and an international arrest warrant remains outstanding for the former CEO. At the time of the tragedy, Union Carbide was one of the largest and most recognizable companies in the world. Today, it's a subsidiary of Dow Chemical.

Similarly, Exxon did nearly everything wrong from a media standpoint during the Valdez oil spill of 1989. One of the most destructive environmental disasters ever, the spill polluted over thirteen hundred square miles of pristine ocean. And even though Exxon launched the most expensive cleanup effort in history, John Devers, then-mayor of Valdez, Alaska, said the community felt "betrayed" by Exxon's response to the crisis. Why? Because Exxon dismissed the concerns of the community, refused to publicly acknowledge the extent of the problem, and accused others of causing delays in the cleanup. Amazingly, Lawrence Rawl,

Exxon's CEO, waited six days before even releasing a statement on the spill. Subsequently, the images people associate with Exxon remain decimated shorelines and dead animals, not the extensive cleanup efforts. In the aftermath of the spill, Exxon's market capitalization plummeted $3 billion, dropping it from the largest oil company in the world to the third largest. As litigation and protests over the Valdez spill continue to this day, Exxon has become the public incarnation of environmentally irresponsible and ecologically destructive corporations.

In a more recent example of reputation mismanagement, the investment bank Lehman Brothers collapsed under the combined weight of poor financial decisions and erroneous public perceptions. Already under stress from the global credit crisis, Lehman allegedly became the target of rumors spread by short sellers and hedge funds. These rumors eroded investor confidence and fueled fears that the investment bank was soon to be sold at an absurdly low price. In a clear PR blunder, Lehman failed to defend its reputation and publicly address the panic surrounding its stock. In the fall of 2008, after nearly 158 years in business, Lehman Brothers filed for what was then the largest bankruptcy in American history.

Bad news situations like industrial accidents, oil spills, and financial impropriety are expected to result in negative headlines and challenging media environments. But, as the following story illustrates, even good news can end up being portrayed as bad news.

When John Walter was anointed CEO of AT&T, it was supposed to be a good news announcement. The company's plan was to introduce Walter to the media and convince stakeholders of his ability to lead AT&T into the future. The event turned out to be anything but good news, and in fact, resulted in a catastrophic outcome. At his introductory news conference, a reporter asked Walter which long-distance provider he used—a valid question considering Walter's new role. Walter was flummoxed, unable to answer a question made relevant by his new position. Within hours of the exchange, AT&T's market capitalization dropped $4 billion.

Clearly, a question about John Walter's service provider does not represent an important strategic or policy issue. However, his inability to answer a simple question had a significant impact on investor confidence. Whether speaking about change in leadership, a poor financial quarter, or a lost championship game, people in the news are under pressure to always have right answers, worded just the right way, knowing they are a slip-of-the-tongue away from harming their share price or becoming a punch line in the *Tonight Show's* opening monologue.

Where's the Rest of What I Said?

When newsmakers see their quotes reported in a less-than-positive fashion, they generally have two lines of defense. The first is "I was misquoted." If that argument fails to sway, then the second line of defense is "I was taken out of context." But what many newsmakers do not realize is that if presented with a hundred sentences, journalists will gravitate to the one sentence, phrase, or quote that paints the story in the light they deem appropriate. Understanding this fact is vital in negotiating the perilous territory of media interaction and avoiding the impact of a negative news story.

You Took Me out of Context

Claiming their remarks were "taken out of context" is a familiar lament for people angry or embarrassed about their quotes in the media. To put context around "out of context," the phrase refers to when reporters get the words right, but change the meaning of what was said. The following exchange represents an example of what could be considered out-of-context reporting:

> *Reporter*: Can you confirm the rumor of mass layoffs in the next quarter?
> *Spokesperson*: There is no truth to the rumor that there will be mass layoffs in the next quarter.

An out-of-context situation would result if the reporter simply quoted the spokesperson as saying, ". . . There will be mass layoffs in the next quarter." Though the spokesperson did in fact use those very words in sequence, the meaning and intent of the quote was changed because the words leading up to it were removed. Out-of-context generally occurs when a journalist isolates particular words in sequence and cuts off words that either precede or follow the quote. In so doing, the journalist changes the meaning of what was said. When this occurs, the victim has every right to defend himself in both a court of law and the court of public opinion. The true problem, however, is that when spokespeople or newsmakers are not hiding behind the "out-of-context" defense, many of them legitimately confuse the editing process with being taken out of context.

It All Comes Down to the Edit

Journalists are gatekeepers who allow viewers, readers, and listeners to see, read, and hear only what they want them to see, read, and hear. The cut and thrust of a media interview is not subject to the rules of everyday chitchat. Normal conversation is free and easy, involving people who alternately talk, listen, pause, reflect, and ask questions stemming from genuine interest or concern. In natural conversation, people are able to appreciate the context of all they hear. That is, if one person delivers ten sentences to another person, then the person listening has a context in which to interpret all they hear. It is therefore helpful for spokespeople to remind themselves that a journalist's job is to separate the wheat from the chaff and sometimes it is only the chaff they seek to report.

Biojax Part 1: The Dynamics of an Interview

What follows is a transcript of an interview from an actual media training session I conducted. The interviewee, Joan Smith (not her real name), is chief executive officer of a biopharmaceutical company I'll call JLA Life Sciences Corporation. Recently, the privately owned company received government approval to market Biojax, a highly effective cancer-fighting biologic drug. Use of the medication is costly. Each round of Biojax treatment costs $25,000. The treatment is only accessible to patients who can afford it and those with insurance plans that cover all or part of the cost of the treatment. So far, government and most managed-care and insurance companies refuse to cover the cost of Biojax treatments. This is despite the fact that Biojax significantly slowed the growth of tumors in 60 percent of patients and demonstrated a clear survival benefit. Going into the media interview, Smith is convinced she has a positive story to tell. Carefully review the interview transcript as it unfolds, because you will have the opportunity to see how the reporter later wrote the story. Here is the unedited media interview:

> *Interviewer*: Biojax is said to be a breakthrough drug in the treatment of various forms of cancer. What is it that makes Biojax effective?
>
> *Joan Smith*: Biojax is a biologic treatment that has a different mechanism of action than traditional cancer medicines. Its anticancer activity is attributed to the general microtubule-destabilizing properties of certain alkaloids.
>
> *Interviewer*: Why is government refusing to cover the cost of Biojax?
>
> *Joan Smith (smiling)*: Well, it's not as if Biojax is dangerous or unproven.
>
> *Interviewer*: Then what is it?
>
> *Joan Smith*: I think it's because government—and this is off the record—but I think government is ignorant when it comes to biologic medicines. Historically, medicines were created using chemicals and compounds and now that we're using living cells, government doesn't have a clue how to value our medicine. So instead of legislating the

necessary guidelines, they're trying to make us look greedy.

Interviewer: Is your company greedy?

Joan Smith: No.

Interviewer: No, what?

Joan Smith: No, we are not greedy.

Interviewer: How do you respond to critics who say that the drug's $25,000 cost rips off cancer patients?

Joan Smith (nodding): It's true that some people are saying that, but they're wrong. We do not rip off cancer patients. (*Fidgeting.*) People say . . . what people don't know . . . we spent hundreds of millions of dollars on research and development for the drug and we need to see a return. I'd like for us to stop talking about the cost of Biojax and start focusing on the drug itself.

Interviewer: Are you gouging cancer patients?

Joan Smith (shifts uncomfortably): I just answered that. No, we are not gouging cancer patients. We even hired a public relations company to help us get that message across.

Interviewer: Yet your company is being blamed for the lack of patient access to the drug because of its high cost. What's your comment?

Joan Smith (crosses arms): You keep asking me the same question over and over again. No, we're not to blame. Pricing a drug like Biojax is complex. Obviously, if anyone is to blame, it's government. Government refuses to pay for the drug because they think we priced it too high. They don't understand that we're in business and a business needs to make money.

Interviewer: Is your company letting people die?

Joan Smith: That question is offensive. No, we are not letting people die.

Interviewer: What were your company's revenues and profits last year?

Joan Smith (forgetting to breathe): We're a privately owned company and I don't have to answer your question.

Interviewer: Is it true that your company is spending $2
    million on its PR and lobbying campaign?
Joan Smith: No comment.
Interviewer: Anything to add?
Joan Smith: No.

Following the interview, which took about two minutes to
conduct, I asked Joan whether the reporter got what he was
looking for and could write a news story based on their encounter. "No, not really," she said. You decide.

Drugmaker Denies "Gouging" Cancer Patients
"We are not greedy," claims CEO

JLA Life Sciences, maker of the recently approved drug Biojax,
is insisting the high-priced oncology treatment "does not rip
off" cancer patients, as critics contend. Biojax, a biologic made
from living cells, is prescribed at a cost of $25,000 per
treatment.

"We are not gouging cancer patients," said Joan Smith,
chief executive officer for the biologic maker. Smith, who denies
the company is "letting people die," blamed government for the
lack of patient access to Biojax. "It's not as if Biojax is
dangerous or unproven," she claimed. "Government refuses to
pay for the drug because they think we priced it too high."

According to JLA's CEO, the problem is that government "is
ignorant when it comes to biologic medicines." Smith blamed
the drug's high cost on research and development expenses.
"We are not greedy," she stated.

She does admit, however, that profit is an important factor
in pricing. "A business needs to make money," she said.

Smith refused to provide specifics when asked about JLA's
revenues and profits. "We're a privately owned company and I
don't have to answer that." She also refused to confirm or deny
that $2 million has been spent on a Biojax public relations
campaign. When asked about the rumor, she snapped, "No
comment."

After sharing this edited news report with Joan, she was in shock. By focusing on the dramatic element in telling her story, did the reporter sensationalize, do something wrong, or act in a less than ethical fashion? No. The quotes are accurate. Like them or not, Joan did make those statements, all of which are truthful. However, she was naturally displeased with the story the reporter wrote. In fact, her initial comment was "You took me out of context. Where's the rest of what I said?"

Please keep this encounter in mind. In Chapter Six, we will revisit the same interview. Only, in the next encounter, Joan will be much better prepared to address criticism of Biojax and begin shaping public perceptions of the drug.

Telling Your Story

When the headline is you, the words out of your mouth can have reverberating consequences. At the same time, a CEO's positive reputation can help drive shareholder value. Edelman Public Relation's Trust Barometer, a yearly comprehensive survey of public sentiment, reports that 90 percent of professional investors are more likely to recommend or buy the stock if the chief executive is seen in a favorable light.[15] The same survey reveals that 93 percent of people find information in articles and news stories more credible than information presented in advertising. Similarly, a study by PR firm Burson-Marsteller found that media is the Number One venue for message delivery. Eighty-four percent of chief executives believe conducting media interviews is the most effective external activity to deliver corporate messages. For comparison, industry conferences and trade shows measured in at close to 62 percent, with advertising at only 47 percent.[16]

What's more, appearing in the media actually contributes to higher executive compensation. A University of Colorado study determined that executives written up in business media earn more money. Study author Markus Fitza interviewed fifteen

Media Goodwill Bank Account

To ensure a positive reputation and build trust, newsmakers need to create what I call a media goodwill bank account. Like any account whose purpose is to build equity, the media goodwill bank account operates best with a positive balance. Positive media relations are like fire insurance, says Canadian columnist Don Martin. "If the home catches fire, it might still burn down, but there's hope of rebuilding from the ashes. With no reservoir of goodwill, newsmakers are fighting a lost cause."[17]

hundred CEOs and concluded that a single article featuring a CEO in the *New York Times*, the *Wall Street Journal*, *Forbes*, *Fortune*, or *BusinessWeek* raised the CEO's compensation by an average of $600,000. In addition, getting on the cover of *Forbes*, *Fortune*, or *BusinessWeek* was good for an average raise of just over $1 million. This type of exposure, he said, leads management and boards of directors to believe their CEOs "had exceptional accomplishments that year."[18] Considering the current social and political climate, this type of positive press coverage is increasingly important.

The Public Is Losing Trust

Today more than ever the general public demands that those they hold accountable be genuine and trustworthy. The previously mentioned Edelman Trust Barometer reveals that the public's trust in corporate leaders is weaker than ever. Edelman reports that trust in U.S. businesses dropped from 58 percent to 38 percent in one year. Outside the United States, businesses in emerging markets received higher numbers, but not by much. The Trust Barometer also found that trust in CEOs as spokespeople fell to an all-time low of 17 percent in the United States.

As discouraging as these numbers seem, they are understandable in a decade defined by the fraud or incompetence of companies like Enron, WorldCom, AIG, and Bear Stearns. Whether due to the S&L crisis of the 1980s, the Long-Term Capital Management bailout in 1998, the dot-com bubble of 2000, or the $700 billion Troubled Asset Relief Program (TARP) created in 2008, corporate and regulatory failures have cost taxpayers trillions of dollars and eroded any sense of public faith in the business leaders and politicians charged with managing capital markets. Clearly, there is a need to build trust and strengthen reputation through positive, proactive interaction with the media. So is media training the answer? Like chicken soup, media training certainly can't hurt, as long as the training teaches spokespeople to truly be responsive.

The Media Training Model Is Broken

Recently, I hosted a media training program with several manufacturing plant managers to help them become better spokespeople. As part of the training, we simulated a fatality at a plant. When I asked Salim, a plant manager, to comment on the death, he responded, "We have an excellent safety record." His safety claim may be true statistically speaking, but this isn't the right moment to gild the lily on safety. Frankly, a worker is dead and Salim's comment about an "excellent safety record" is not appropriate given the situation. Besides, the comment is defensive and fails to acknowledge the emotions surrounding what has taken place.

When I asked Salim why he answered as he did, he told me a media trainer had instructed him to only provide reporters with positive messages, regardless of the question. Regrettably, this was another in a long list of instances of media trainers telling spokespeople to ignore reporters' questions and just get out their messages. The current model for media training is broken because it calls on spokespeople to ignore questions and simply repeat so-called "key" messages. Each time a nonresponsive message is repeated, a layer of trustworthiness is stripped away from the speaker. The delivery of predetermined messages, regardless of questions asked, whittles away at the spokesperson's credibility. Given a spokesperson's objective is to build trust with the media, it doesn't make sense to chip away at that trust with messages that never really answer questions.

In learning to be better media communicators, spokespeople and executives must not be encouraged to be slick and polished. People do not trust slick and polished. Instead, the objectives of media training should be to learn how to directly address difficult questions, how to avoid falling into media traps, and most importantly, how to accomplish the two previous tasks with honesty and integrity.

In my experience, media training can only be truly effective if executives are aggressively challenged and questioned. Few other people will talk to executives in the probing, confrontational way a journalist may. This can be disconcerting. Unfortunately, many executives feel they do not need to practice answering questions until a crisis occurs and a reporter is knocking on their door. Then, and only then, do they take the process seriously. But the process of interrogating executives in practice sessions has value, if for no other reason than to subject them to the types of tough questions that only journalists have the audacity to ask.

While a book, a seminar, or an online tutorial cannot expose you to the stress of a contentious interview or packed news conference, the remaining chapters in this book will provide an effective alternative to the broken media training model. One that offers strategies for navigating all types of media events with expertise and integrity. One that will help you address confrontational questions while still delivering proactive and positive messages. And, subsequently, one that will help you avoid the many gaffes, missteps, and blunders that inevitably lead to a media catastrophe.

Chapter Talking Points

- Reporters look for dramatic situations with compelling characters. These types of stories are easy to write and simple for readers to understand.

- News stories usually fall into categories such as good versus evil, winners and losers, bad decisions, irony, rumors, the unusual or absurd, offensive comments, uninformed politicians, and failed jokes.

- Hero, villain, victim, survivor, and village idiot are some of the stock characters that reporters use to write their stories quickly.

- Journalists are influenced by unconscious personal biases as well as the stress of constant deadlines.

- With the explosion of social media, companies must continually monitor and respond to what is being written about them. Wait too long and an organization's reputation might be irreparably harmed.

- Reporters edit interview quotes for dramatic impact and to get to the essence of an issue.

- An edited quote is not the same as one that has been taken out of context.

- The current model for media training is broken because it calls on spokespeople to ignore questions and repeat "key" messages. Each time a nonresponsive message is repeated, a layer of credibility is stripped away from the speaker.

- The most effective way to deal with the media is to be honest and responsive.

2

YOU ARE THE STORY

"When the satellite TV truck has pulled into the corporate parking lot, it is too late to discuss crisis management."
—*Howard Paster, CEO of Hill and Knowlton*

Picking up the phone and discovering there's a journalist on the other end of the line can cause your heart to skip a beat, making it potentially easy to say something inappropriate and newsworthy. It's a natural reaction. Unless you've just won a Nobel Prize or an Academy Award, rarely does a journalist call because it's good news. I've personally witnessed the darting eyes, sweat-soaked shirt, and trembling voice of a newsmaker or spokesperson caught off-guard by an unexpected inquiry. But how you manage this initial encounter may very well determine whether the ensuing media interaction will be a success or a failure. It will be your first chance to dispel rumors or address controversy. It will be an opportunity to begin shaping the resulting news story and influencing public perception. In this chapter, you will learn how to manage the initial encounter with a journalist, avoid common interview traps, and align your organizational image with positive values.

When Reporters Make Contact

Unless you proactively seek media coverage, most interview encounters begin with a phone call from a reporter. From the instant you answer the phone to the instant you get off the phone, everything you say could be on the front page of tomorrow's paper. Therefore, the initial phone call or confrontation requires a basic strategy for managing surprise inquiries, as well as a clear understanding of the rules that govern media interaction with the public. When a journalist calls or confronts you in your company's lobby, follow this simple three-step strategy:

1. Be Friendly

When a reporter asks for an interview, the reporter can sense whether you want to talk or not. If the reporter hears stress, irritation, or anxiety in your voice, it could be an immediate tip-off that you may be less than cooperative and may, in fact, have something to hide. When you're involved in a controversial incident, the reporter invariably expects you to be defensive upon contact. The conversation that follows is almost certain to move in a negative direction based simply on the tense, impatient tone of your voice. To reduce this possibility, try to sound as friendly as possible. By sounding friendly, you will convey a desire to be helpful and forthcoming. In many cases, when a reporter is looking for a villain or "village idiot" to anchor a story, she may be thrown off by a friendly and cooperative demeanor. When I was a reporter, if someone I was hoping to vilify responded in a warm and friendly manner, I immediately considered trying to find someone else to interview.

Are You Newsworthy?

Here are a few of the elements that help determine whether a situation might indeed be newsworthy:

- Has there been a rare accident? (bridge collapse in Minnesota)
- Has an act of nature occurred, the likes of which have rarely been seen before? (tsunami in Southeast Asia)

- Has something happened for the first time ever? (Octomom)
- Has an important person made an announcement that touches the lives of many? (sending more troops to Iraq)
- Is new information coming forward that provides people with news they can use or that will benefit them in their everyday lives? (More than two alcoholic beverages a day could increase the risk of cancer.)
- Has somebody famous done or been accused of having done something wrong? (the Tiger Woods sex scandal)
- Is there a significant event that has taken or will take place? (the passing of health care reform)
- Has the reporter learned information no one else is aware of? (Vice President Dick Cheney accidentally shoots a fellow quail hunter.)
- Has the reporter obtained a visual no one else has seen before? (Prince Harry in a Nazi uniform)

It's natural to be nervous when speaking with a journalist, but that doesn't mean you need to sound nervous. To sound friendly, use a conversational vocal inflection. This means trying to talk as you do when you are engaged in a relaxed, enjoyable conversation. One very effective way to make your voice sound more conversational is to use your hands when you talk. In Chapter Five, I provide a number of other techniques to help you seem relaxed in stressful situations, so be sure to review those as you practice sounding genial and forthcoming. Once you have presented a friendly, relaxed persona to the reporter, move on to Step Two.

2. Create a Buffer Zone

Though the reporter wants you to drop everything and be interviewed right now, you are entitled to a couple of moments to gather your thoughts. Tell the reporter, "I'm just in the middle of something right now"—which you no doubt are, even if it's playing solitaire. Then add, "Please tell me how I can be of service and I will do my best to help." You should never do an interview with the media or provide a reporter with meaningful quotes until you know the proposed content and context of the story.

If the reporter hesitates to provide appropriate information on the story, be very careful. A reporter may not tell you the true or entire purpose of the intended story if he thinks full disclosure would kill the opportunity for an interview. For example, while investigating nursing homes during my reporting days, I told the administrator of one home that the purpose of my interview was to shed light on what life was like for seniors in these facilities. In actual fact, my purpose was to get the administrator's reaction to allegations of resident abuse. If I had told her that, however, I never would have been invited into the home. To be true to my word, the first ten minutes of the interview were dedicated to general questions about life in a nursing home. Then, when the administrator's guard was down, I hit her with questions about residents suffering abuse and malnutrition.

More often than not, though, a reporter will tell you the true purpose of the call. Generally, reporters avoid lying in order to get a story. They know they'll have to answer for it later, either to their editor or a judge. But there is a lot of wiggle room between "tell the truth" and "don't lie." If you are unprepared to be questioned or do not have a complete understanding of what the journalist is looking for, be sure not to answer questions that could be problematic. Instead, move on to Step Three.

3. Ask the Reporter Questions

Although reporters make their living asking questions, it often benefits you to reverse roles and ask a series of questions of your own. The answers you get to these initial questions will provide insight into the content and context of the proposed interview and the resulting news story. If you sense the reporter is hesitant to answer your questions, it may be because the reporter is holding back and wants to surprise you with a question or issue you aren't expecting. In that initial call or contact, ask the following questions to determine the needs of the journalist and pay careful attention to what she tells you—or doesn't tell you.

When talking to a **print or newspaper reporter**, ask:

- What's the purpose of the interview? (Let the reporter explain why she contacted you.)

- When will the article be published? (Provides you with a sense of timing.)

- What's the article's overall objective? (Meant to give you insight into the end result the reporter is looking for and ensure the objective is in keeping with the purpose of the interview.)

- Who else are you interviewing? (Know who else will be quoted. If the reporter refuses to answer, you should hear alarm bells.)

- What section of the paper is the article for? (Know the audience—is it for the news section, the business section, or the style section?)

- Are you interested in reporting on ____? (Fill in the blank with a topic that benefits you. It's possible you can help shape the story by providing information the journalist was, up to now, unaware of.)

- How much time do you need for the interview and where do you want to do it? (If the reporter says she needs thirty to sixty minutes, then your information will play a prominent role in the story. Doing the interview on your own turf provides an opportunity to influence the setting and tone.)

- What's your deadline? (I always told people my deadline was sooner than it actually was to pressure them into responding faster.)

- What's your phone number and e-mail address so I can get back to you? (When you are the one to initiate the response or callback, it is easier to influence the flow of conversation and end it at the appropriate time.)

While most of the questions for TV or radio reporters are the same, there are a few critical differences between the broadcast and print mediums. Generally speaking, TV is more intimate and revealing. Seeing a person run away from a TV camera has greater impact than reading about it. If you refuse to talk to a TV reporter, all she has to do is barge into your office or show up on your front step to get visuals of you refusing to talk, covering your face, or trying to push away the camera. All of these images make for compelling TV. Likewise, there is a greater immediacy to TV news. CNN, FOX News, and other all-news outlets are starved for content. As such, they are in constant search of images. And with the popularity of YouTube, any gaffe that is captured on camera lives on the Web in perpetuity. So in a sense, more is at risk when you either participate in or refuse to do a television interview. With that in mind, following is a list of questions to ask a broadcast journalist.

When talking to a **TV or radio reporter**, ask:

- What's the purpose of the interview? (Let the reporter explain why she contacted you.)
- When will the story be broadcast? (Provides you with a sense of timing.)
- What's the segment's overall objective? (Meant to give you insight into the end result the reporter is looking for and ensure the objective is in keeping with the purpose of the interview.)
- Who else are you interviewing? (Know who else will be contacted. If the reporter refuses to answer, you should hear alarm bells.)

- Will the interview be "live" or "taped"? (Taped interviews can be edited to fit the reporter's perspective.)

- Is the interview for a ninety-second news report or is it for a longer feature? (For shorter segments, you need more focused and quotable messages.)

- Are you interested in reporting on ____? (Fill in the blank with a topic that benefits you. It's possible you can begin shaping the story by providing information the journalist was, up to now, unaware of.)

- How much time do you need for the interview and where do you want to do it? (Lengthy interviews offer more opportunities for mistakes. Doing the interview on your own turf provides an opportunity to influence the setting and tone.)

- What's your deadline? (I always told people my deadline was sooner than it actually was to pressure them into responding faster.)

- What's your phone number and e-mail address so I can get back to you? (When you are the one to initiate the response or callback, it is easier to influence the flow of conversation and end it at the appropriate time.)

When you ask reporters to tell you about their story, frame each question from the perspective of wanting to help. If you simply say, "What's the purpose of the interview?" the reporter can write, "'What's the purpose of the interview,' barked an irritated Ansell." Better to say, "I want to appreciate the scope of the story—please help me understand the purpose of the interview." Or, "To help me understand the breadth of the story, please share with me who else you'll be interviewing." That way, your questions will not sound like an interrogation.

If the reporter will not let you off the phone in that initial call and persistently fires questions at you, tell her, "The sooner I wrap up what I'm doing, the sooner I can get back to you with all the information you need." Then, once you have the information needed to answer her questions and highlight your own agenda, get back to the reporter at a designated time. If the designated time passes, call or e-mail the reporter with an update.

When you do call back, "winging it" is not advisable—even if you consider yourself a skilled public speaker. Giving presentations and answering questions from the media are two very different situations. Questions and comments cannot always be predicted, and as helpful as the gift of gab may be it is not nearly enough to succeed during a media interaction. The gift of gab can actually work against you, especially if you aren't extremely careful with what you say or don't completely understand the meaning of journalistic terms like "off the record."

Be Careful What You Say

When a reporter is on the phone, every word is fair game for a quote. This means you can count on the reporter combing through what you say very carefully for something, anything, to get his story printed. For example, consider the following fictional telephone exchange:

> *Reporter:* I'm working on a story about rumored layoffs at your plants.
> *Spokesperson:* So you want to talk about rumors of layoffs.
> *Reporter:* I also want to talk about the rumor that you've lost the government funding you were hoping for.
> *Spokesperson:* So you also want to talk about a rumor that we have lost our funding.
> *Reporter:* I would also like you to comment on the possibility your CEO and CFO may be fired by the board of directors.
> *Spokesperson:* And you want to talk about the board possibly firing the CEO and CFO.

In this brief exchange, look at the words the spokesperson used by merely repeating what the reporter asked:

- ". . . rumors of layoffs"
- ". . . we have lost our funding"
- ". . . possibly firing the CEO and CFO"

The reporter now has numerous options for piecing together a dramatic headline to splash across the front page of tomorrow's business section. Here is a better way for a spokesperson to handle this conversation:

> *Reporter:* I'm working on a story about rumored layoffs at your plants.
> *Spokesperson:* So you want to talk about our workforce.
> *Reporter:* I also want to talk about the rumor that you've lost the government funding you were hoping for.
> *Spokesperson:* So you also want to talk about funding.
> *Reporter:* I would also like you to comment on the possibility your CEO and CFO may be fired by the board of directors.
> *Spokesperson:* And you want to talk about our executive team.

In this exchange, the spokesperson has acknowledged the reporter's questions in a responsive and accommodating way, but without providing the reporter with quotable information. Remember, everything you say in that opening conversation can be reported by the journalist. Therefore, always be very careful.

The Truth About "Off the Record"

"Off the record" is a journalism term that means a statement is not for publication or attribution. Although there is controversy surrounding the origins of the term, it certainly has been popularized in movies and TV dramas. These fictional depictions have led people to believe that journalists follow a strict set of rules when it comes to sourcing material and dealing with the public. The fact is there are no definitive rules and nothing is ever truly "off the record." Many people have been burned thinking otherwise. If you're not certain whether to share specific information with journalists, follow this simple credo—when in doubt, leave it out.

If you're determined to ignore the above advice, only agree to go off the record with a reporter you absolutely trust to keep your remarks off tonight's newscast or out of tomorrow's newspaper. But unless you're really certain, that's a big chance to take. If you do tell a reporter that your comments are off the record, at least do so before you offer the comments. Off the record is not retroactive. The following is a great example of a savvy and successful businessman who believed the "off-the-record" myth.

Drug company owner Barry Sherman was interviewed by Leslie Stahl of 60 *Minutes*. Stahl's story was about a medical researcher who claimed to be a victim of a smear campaign by Sherman's company. Here's a partial transcript of Stahl's report:

Sherman: She (the researcher) is the one who is conducting the smear campaign.

Leslie Stahl (voiceover): But when we changed the tapes, he changed his tune, unaware that the cameras were rolling again.

Stahl: Let me finish this and then we'll go back. . . .

Sherman: She's nuts. Nuts.

Stahl: What did you just say to me? You just said she was nuts. You just said that to me. You looked at me and you said she was nuts.

Sherman: I said to you. . . .

Stahl: You said she's nuts.

Sherman: Hold on a sec. I said I'll say certain things to you off the record. . . .

Stahl: Yes, but that wasn't off the record. We were rolling. The cameras were going. The point is that you are still saying these things and I am a reporter.

Sherman: I am obviously very upset and given that I'm upset I might well say things that in a private conversation, off the record, that I would not say on. . . .

Stahl: Yes, but we're reporters. We're not your pals.

Commenting on Sherman's encounter with Stahl, journalist John Fraser was less than kind to his colleagues: "Journalists can be good and decent people just like any other professionals. They can also be perfect shits."[1]

Image Consciousness

Corporate image involves how consumers perceive the corporate entity behind the brands it markets or the services it provides. A positive image helps sell product. It boosts share price and influences public trust. A positive corporate image greatly increases brand equity and brand adoption. In short, image matters to a company's bottom line. So much so that, according to a comprehensive eMarketer report compiled by David Hallerman, corporations and organizations in the United States spend in excess of $250 billion per year on advertising to help shape their image.[2] But a corporation's image is not solely created by the company. Other contributors to a company's image include consumers, journalists, bloggers, and advocacy groups. Therefore, when a reporter calls or a crisis occurs, it's important to know what others are saying about your organization and to be aware of how you come across in the court of public opinion.

Know What Others Are Saying About You

To help manage your organization's reputation, you should troll the Web to identify what, if anything, is being said about you and who is saying it. Although monitoring the myriad sites that could be talking about you is a monumental task, google.com is a good place to start. Free blog search tools can help, too. They include blogsearch.google.com; technorati.com, which searches for user-generated media (including blogs) by tag or keyword; and blogpulse.com, which analyzes and reports on daily activity in the blogosphere. Other sites helpful to search beyond blogs include search.twitter.com and uservoice.com.

In all searches, look for keywords connected to your business or the names of your products and add words like "sucks," "blows," and "stinks." You may not like what you find. Brian Solis of Future Works discovered two-thousand-plus Web domains that ended with the phrase ". . . stinks.com." Some organizations beat critics to the punch and actually purchase domains with their company name followed by the words "sucks" or "stinks."

Many successful companies see the value in actively following and managing their image. For instance, when consumers posted negative blogs accusing Dell of having poor customer service, the computer company created IdeaStorm, a website where unhappy Dell users could post their problems, share ideas with the company, and even help other customers. The company succeeded in cutting the number of negative blog posts from 49 percent to 22 percent.[3]

With the widespread use of the Web and the emergence of social media, even companies innocent of wrongdoing can become victims of negative publicity. Jamba Juice is a California-based company that advertises its "healthy blended beverages, juices, and good-for-you-snacks." So when a blog known as *The Consumerist* reported that Jamba Juice used milk in its nondairy smoothies, an outcry was unleashed. The blog posting was linked to twenty other blogs and read twenty-three thousand times. It turned out that the information was incorrect. Jamba Juice called *The Consumerist* to say the information was wrong but did not post anything on its own website.

The Consumerist did correct the story on its blog, but the accusation against Jamba Juice was viewed by six times as many people as the correction.[4] Had Jamba Juice paid more attention to blog reports about one of its products, it could have minimized the damage to its reputation. "A lie can travel halfway around the world, while the truth is still putting on its shoes," Mark Twain said more than a century ago. Consider the relevance of his statement in today's connected world.

Know How You Come Across

Simply focusing on what to say when there is controversy serves only to distract spokespeople from addressing the larger question of how they want to be seen by the audiences they care about—shareholders, customers, suppliers, bankers, employees, and the public. With these stakeholders, there is little to gain by appearing in the media as defensive, argumentative, or unresponsive. Even Steven Jobs, considered one of the most visionary business leaders of our time, has faltered when pressed by a persistent journalist.

Several years ago, Jobs's company Apple was rudderless without a CEO. CNBC offered Jobs an interview, which provided him with an opportunity to boost investor confidence. Before the live on-air interview began, Jobs told the interviewer he did not want to talk about the search for a new Apple CEO. Did he truly believe that by telling a reporter he didn't want to talk about something, the reporter would stay off the subject? If anything, it makes the question more tempting because it obviously touches a nerve. After a few questions about foreign markets, the interviewer predictably turned to the prohibited topic:

Interviewer: Okay, and the other area everyone wants to know about is the CEO search. What's the status there?

Jobs: We're going along as planned and we're continuing to look.

Interviewer: The perception is the short list has been exhausted, and out of the good choices a couple of good candidates slipped through your fingers. Is the search in disarray right now?

Jobs: Well, you see, you should talk to them if you think they know. I . . . it's a very different view.

Interviewer: I think a lot of people do think it's not going too well. Is that an incorrect perception?

Jobs: It's not my perception.

Interviewer: Have you ruled out totally the idea of taking the job?

Jobs: We agreed we weren't going to talk about that.

Jobs then whips off his lavaliere microphone, flicks it away, gets up, and leaves the set live, on the air.

Interviewer: All right, Steve, thank you very much. Steven Jobs live from San Francisco.

The CNBC encounter with Jobs made for compelling TV. Investors and analysts watched Jobs come across as angry and petulant—not a good way to project himself, especially in front of the international investment community. Apple's stock price dropped almost 30 percent in the following month, closing at a split-adjusted low of $3.23 per share.

Building Trust

Knowing how you want to be perceived is a critical starting point for both answering questions when a controversial situation arises and shaping an overall, long-term media strategy. Clearly, there is much to be gained by projecting an image of openness, honesty, and empathy. Much of your success in conveying these qualities and influencing public perception depends on tone. Following are the stories of two companies caught in a public controversy over offensive advertising campaigns. The first company is Dairy Queen, a leading restaurant chain specializing in ice cream. The second company is Tim Hortons, a coffee and donut chain.

The offending Dairy Queen ad featured a boy flailing on a hook that hung on the back of a door while his older brother laughed and ate ice cream. The ad was not funny to the Neuts family, whose ten-year-old son Miles died after being hung on a hook at school. The family approached the company, demanding the ad be pulled. When Dairy Queen refused, the boy's father called for a North American–wide boycott of the ice cream chain. Finally, Dairy Queen agreed to pull the commercial in the town where the Neuts family lived.[5]

Contrast Dairy Queen's handling of the situation with the response that Tim Hortons offered in a controversy it faced. Free coffee mugs were the giveaway in the "Get Mugged with Tim Hortons" contest, but the play on words did not sit well with the family of Erin Sperrey, who had been beaten to death while on the night shift at the Tim Hortons in Caribou, Maine. Erin's mother sent Tim Hortons an e-mail: "I am appalled that you would dare use a reference to violence in your advertising campaign. If you are going to do that, why don't you go all the way and make it, 'Get Mugged and Murdered with Tim Hortons?'"[6]

A typical or traditional PR response to this kind of controversy may have been, "It wasn't our intention to offend anyone. Our mug contest is simply a fun promotion." Instead, company spokesman Nick Javor recognized the depth of feeling and personally apologized to the family and then publicly apologized. "It was a poor choice of words for a promotion anywhere," said Javor. "We feel awful."

In the first example, Dairy Queen disregarded the Neuts family tragedy and came across as arrogant and indifferent. The company's denial incited a public dispute that nearly resulted in a significant loss of reputation and business. Tim Hortons, in contrast, responded in a way that made the company appear responsive and humane. Its compassionate handling of the controversy led to a swift resolution that drew praise from victim advocacy groups. How did Tim Hortons decide to take this tack? They asked themselves one of the most important questions to consider when managing a public relations crisis.

What's the Right Thing to Do?

In counseling clients in crisis, there is one question I always ask: "Money aside and lawyers aside, what's the right thing to do?" This is all the more important when people suffer or experience harm as a result of an action by a company. In such situations, it is vital that corporate figureheads take responsibility for their company's mistakes and fix them. That question and the answer that went with it were front and center in the work I did with PG&E in what has come to be known as the Erin Brockovich case.

In the 1950s, '60s, and '70s, Pacific Gas & Electric, the California utility that is a subsidiary of PG&E Corporation, used chromium, a rust inhibitor, in cooling towers at gas compressor stations in remote parts of its service area. Wastewater containing the chromium was put into unlined pools at those sites. The practice was both common and legal.

Over the years, the chromium made its way into the groundwater in those areas, contaminating the drinking water supply. Some PG&E employees became aware of the problem in the 1960s, but they did not share the information with others in the company or with the public. Years later, in the late 1980s, a number of families came forward, insisting they were suffering high rates of disease, which were later blamed on their exposure to chromium. They filed a class-action lawsuit against PG&E.

The right thing to do in the Erin Brockovich situation, at the very least, was to acknowledge the suffering of members of the community. However, in situations of this nature, most lawyers instinctively want to put up a wall and not go anywhere near acknowledging the pain, suffering, or inconvenience others may have experienced due to something the company may or may not have done, even if the alleged misdeed took place a generation ago.

The leadership in place at the time when the Erin Brockovich case came to the fore recognized the need to confront the situation in a manner that displayed sensitivity to the concerns of community members. Even though they were not convinced that the company was responsible for ailments in the community, PG&E's leaders, along with the company's public affairs executives, wanted their messaging to reflect an empathetic tone.

After the plaintiffs secured a settlement from PG&E, company chairman and CEO Peter Darbee said it was important to "act with integrity and communicate honestly and openly." Darbee's words matched his values. "We know this case has been difficult and emotional for the plaintiffs and their families," he said. "We are accountable for all of our own actions; these include safety, protecting the environment, and supporting our communities." Darbee went on to say, "This situation should never have happened and we are sorry that it did. It is not the way we do business, and I believe it would not happen in our company today" (Peter Darbee, e-mail message to employees, February 3, 2006). With those heartfelt words, Peter Darbee acknowledged the community's hardship and earned the trust of his stakeholding public on a very emotional issue.

Getting General Counsel on Your Side

Getting lawyers to consider organizational credibility and trust can be tough when their primary focus is to protect the company from excessive liability. Here is a ten-step process to get general counsel on your side:

1. Tell legal counsel that organizational credibility, long-term reputation, and trust must be considered.
2. Ask important players in the room how they want the company to be perceived by key stakeholders.
3. Ask the lawyer to help lead the group through a process to identify answers and messages.
4. Respectfully ask the lawyer the tough questions that need answers, such as "Did your product harm people?"
5. Have everyone in the room take good notes on the answers the lawyer suggests.
6. When the answers are complete, thank the lawyer and remind the group how the company wants to be seen by its stakeholders.
7. Ask the lawyer if she believes the answers reflect the way the company wants to be perceived by its stakeholders.
8. If the lawyer believes her answers are fine (and you believe otherwise) ask the group its opinion.
9. If the lawyer's answers do not reflect the way the company wants to be perceived, ask the lawyer what could be said instead.
10. Steer discussion of the answers back to your original suggestion, adding words of value provided by the lawyer.

Today, more companies and organizations are moving toward this open, empathetic approach. When it turned out that Biogen Idec's potential blockbuster drug for multiple sclerosis, Tysabri, may have been responsible for a rare brain disease in three patients, CEO James C. Mullen alerted the FDA, suspended sales, and initiated a review of all three thousand patients in its clinical trials. "Here was a risk that we didn't understand," said Mullen. "Stopping the drug was the right thing to do."[7]

Sometimes, doing the right thing can involve going against conventional wisdom. Even when his trucking company clients are clearly liable in fatal road accidents, Tennessee lawyer Jim

Golden reaches out to family members of victims "just to say we're sorry for your loss." Though his legal colleagues claim such an action will damage their negotiating position, Golden says it helps to "break the wall of silence." The result has been a profound reduction in the number of claims and the cost of claims, with some of his clients achieving 20 to 30 percent savings in insurance premiums. One large company that manufactures products such as lawn mowers has saved $50 million on product liability claims and $6 million in insurance premiums since adopting this more open approach.

The one constant in all of these examples is that each company or organization elected to take responsibility for its mistake regardless of costs or damages. Doing so was especially meaningful when lives were at stake. Unfortunately, doing the right thing can be an elusive concept, particularly during times of crisis. But all of these companies chose to do the right thing and subsequently enhanced their credibility by matching their actions, policies, and messages to a set of fundamental values.

Look to Your Values

Managing your image and reputation in difficult times requires firmly held values brought to life by words and actions. A focus on values illuminates ways to build confidence with stakeholders, especially when managing issues of high concern and low trust. Recalibrating to fundamental values will lead you to pathways that offer clarity on what needs to be said and done.

When Nancy Daigneault became president of mychoice.ca, a Canadian smokers' rights group, she knew she was in for criticism, not only from media and special interest groups but also from friends and family. Mychoice.ca is funded by tobacco companies, which are about as popular as pigs at a bar mitzvah.

Daigneault, a nonsmoker, said the website would give voice to the concerns of Canadian smokers, who face growing government smoking bans as well as personal demonization. "Smokers have the same rights as everyone else to be consulted and to have their concerns taken into account—but you wouldn't know it from the way they are treated," said Daigneault. "Banks, businesses, professions, and all kinds of different groups in society are able to influence public policy by banding together and speaking out clearly to make sure politicians cannot ignore their concerns," Daigneault said. "Why shouldn't Canada's five million adult smokers be able to do the same?" The mychoice.ca website would not promote smoking but rather would provide links to quit-smoking programs. "I am a former smoker who quit because of the health risks involved and would not be part of anything that encouraged people to smoke," she said.

When the Ontario Medical Association called for a ban on smoking in cars carrying kids, Daigneault was invited to comment on an afternoon radio show. Going into the interview, she knew there were three messages she wanted to deliver:

- "No one would advocate smoking in cars with kids."
- "Smokers care about and love their children just as much as nonsmokers and should take this advice."
- "Public education is a better way to let smokers know they shouldn't smoke in cars carrying kids."

Daigneault's advisers did not want her to deliver the first message. They felt that saying no one would advocate smoking in a car with kids would confirm that a problem actually exists. Uncomfortable with the advice, Daigneault took it anyway. As a result, she came across in a manner that suggested she actually supported smoking in cars with kids. "I became somewhat defensive and probably sounded angry during the interview," she told me later. "After the interview, I told my advisers that I would, in subsequent interviews, deliver message number one. Later that day, I did at least ten other interviews and delivered all the messages I wanted to deliver and the interviews were fine. Without the first message, I sounded like a crazy person who thought it was okay to smoke with kids in the car."

As Daigneault discovered, it can be a mistake to abandon one's values in the face of controversy. This is particularly true in situations that present a clear moral or ethical position. Obviously, smoking in cars when children are present is one such issue; it really doesn't have two sides to it. While Daigneault's mistake was easily corrected by readjusting her message to fit her values, it could have just as easily been avoided. As she later admitted, "I didn't pull out my Value Compass and I got a bit burned."

The Value Compass

The Value Compass, pictured in Figure 2.1, is a powerful tool to help you deal with public battles and situations that are unlikely to be won in the court of public opinion. When the public's trust is threatened, the compass is a guide or road map to meaningful, honest responses that present you and your organization in a positive way.

There are three basic components of the Value Compass: the blank "stakeholders" line near the top of the form, the actual "compass" and its four corresponding directions, and the four blank spaces above the "NEWS" acronym at the bottom. The "stakeholder(s)" line is used to identify the people most affected by the news event in question. The compass itself indicates four directions, or categories, presented on two primary axes. The north-south axis represents the (N)ature and (S)tandards of the spokesperson and her organization. These two categories help the spokesperson identify the image and traits her organization wants to project to the media and public. The east-west axis, in contrast, represents the (E)motions and (W)ell-being of stakeholders. Identifying and understanding the perspective of stakeholders helps you in framing responsive messages and matching future actions to stakeholder needs. Three words should

Figure 2.1 The Value Compass

Value Compass

Stakeholder(s)

N NATURE

WELL-BEING W   STAKE HOLDERS   E EMOTIONS

SPOKESPERSON

STANDARDS S

N	E	W	S
Spokesperson's Nature	Stakeholder's Emotion	Stakeholder's Well-being	Spokesperson's Standards

© Jeff Ansell 2010

be selected for each category. Then, from these three words, one word that best applies to the current news event should be chosen and placed in the appropriate blank at the bottom. Once in place, all decisions, actions, and communications are screened through the "NEWS" filter created by these four Value Compass terms.

Table 2.1 Value Compass Words

Nature	Emotions	Well-being	Standards
Authentic	Anger	Action	Articulate
Compassionate	Disappointment	Comfort	Credible
Empathetic	Frustration	Education	Ethical
Honest	Optimism	Health	Reliable
Sincere	Relief	Security	Trustworthy

If this all sounds a bit overwhelming, don't worry. Detailed, step-by-step directions for creating your own Value Compass follow a little later in this chapter. In addition, an abridged set of directions is included with the blank Value Compass in the Messaging Tool Kit in the Appendix. Sometimes thinking of appropriate Value Compass words can be challenging, so I've provided a list of the twenty words most echoed by clients in my practice for each category. Table 2.1 shows a partial list of these terms. For the complete list, see the Appendix.

Of course, this is only a guide. When you create your own Value Compass, use any words you find most applicable to your specific circumstances. Key words from your organization's mission or vision statement often work well. The terms I provide here should be considered a starting point as you determine how you want to be perceived by the media and public. To create your own Value Compass, use the following step-by-step instructions.

Value Compass Instructions

Step 1: Start by filling in the blank "stakeholder(s)" line. Your stakeholders are the people most affected by your news or the people you hope to reach with your message. If you are responding to an industrial accident, your stakeholders might be accident victims, employees affected by the accident, or concerned local citizens. If your news is a disappointing revenue report, your stakeholders are likely the board of directors or company shareholders. To differentiate between various possibilities, think about whom you will be addressing. If you are speaking at a board of directors meeting, the board will be your stakeholders. But if you are being interviewed on CNBC, your stakeholders will be shareholders and institutional investors.

Step 2: Next, begin filling in the north-south axis. This is the "spokesperson" axis that comprises (N)ature and (S)tandards. Start with (N)ature. By nature, I mean the characteristics, including ways of thinking and feeling, you want to present to the public. These are usually adjectives that describe organic or instinctive parts of your identity and personality. Are you open, empathetic, and understanding? Are you caring or humble? Keep in mind, these words need to correspond to the issue, situation, or news event in question. For example, if you are preparing a Value Compass to help develop a messaging strategy for an oil spill, using words like "cheerful" and "lighthearted" would be inappropriate. Write down three adjectives that come to mind or choose three appropriate terms from the provided word list.

Step 3: Once you decide on three words to describe your nature, move to the blank lines for (S)tandards. Broadly speaking, standards refer to a set of requirements, ideals, or a model of excellence. More specifically, standards should be exceptional principles and practices you wish to project to the public. Do you want to be seen as trustworthy, accountable, and credible? Or, do you want to be seen as competent, articulate, and professional? Sometimes people have trouble distinguishing between nature and standards. The key difference is that the former is an inherent quality ("We're open and caring"), while the latter is a standard or ideal that you and your organization strive to achieve ("We work to be professional and reliable"). Another way to think of it is that nature represents inner qualities that your organization wants to project, while standards represent external criteria that you and your organization try to live up to. Again, be sure to use words that correspond to the issue, situation, or news event in question.

Step 4: Next, move to the "stakeholders" axis. Start by identifying your stakeholders' (E)motions. To do this, try imagining the feelings and reactions created by your issue or news event. If there was an industrial accident, have colleagues and loved ones been lost? If so, stakeholders could be angry, sad, or fearful. If there was a poor business result, board members and investors are likely to feel surprise, disappointment, and frustration. With a good news event, stakeholders may feel pride, awe, and optimism. In choosing emotions, it is best to pick words that represent a range of feelings rather than words that are closely linked. For example, anger and sadness are very different emotions. In contrast, sadness, depression, and despondency—though subtly different in meaning—all refer to a state of unhappiness. By choosing a range of emotions, you will develop a more complete, multidimensional picture of your stakeholders and their perspective.

Step 5: After identifying your stakeholders' emotions, determine what it will take to enhance or ensure their (W)ell-being. What can you and your organization do to address their emotions, concerns, and needs? In the industrial accident example, this may involve action, comfort, and security. After a bad quarter, board members may need commitment, performance, and profit. If you have trouble thinking of "well-being" terms, refer to the list of Value Compass Words in the Appendix. Pick three applicable terms from the list or use it as a catalyst to help you think of more suitable terms.

Step 6: Once you have filled in three words for each direction, work through the categories again and choose one term from each that best reflects your desired image and your stakeholders' perspective. This process should be done in a slightly different order than filling in the initial categories. For this step, start with (N)ature, then do (E)motion, next do (W)ell-being, and finish with (S)tandards.

There is a simple reason for this change. In earlier steps, working on each axis separately allows you to adopt the spokesperson's mind-set, then the stakeholders' mind-set. Keeping each mind-set distinct at this point will help you avoid overlap or repetition between categories. But since the point now is to choose four words that work well collectively, a cross-axis approach is best. Start with the spokesperson axis (N), move to the stakeholder axis (E and W), then return to the spokesperson axis (S). By alternating between axes, it will be easier for you to correlate the image you project with the emotions and needs of your stakeholders.

Starting with the spokesperson axis, what (N)ature word best addresses your news event? Then, shifting to the stakeholder axis, what is their primary (E)motion? Next, what do they most need to ensure or enhance their (W)ell-being? This will usually be the action or attitude that best addresses the primary emotion you chose. Once you have established these terms, return to the spokesperson axis. What (S)tandard best addresses or complements the (N)ature, (E)motion, and (W)ell-being terms you have already chosen? As you select a word from each category, write it in the appropriate blank at the bottom. These four words now constitute a "NEWS" filter to use as you create media messages and prepare to address the public.

Figure 2.2 presents a completed Value Compass created by a recent client of mine. Working in a controversial industry within the consumer staples sector, this client was accused of tax evasion and pled guilty to a $200 million fine. To help deal with upcoming public relations events, the company's director of corporate affairs created the following Value Compass:

Figure 2.2 Client Value Compass

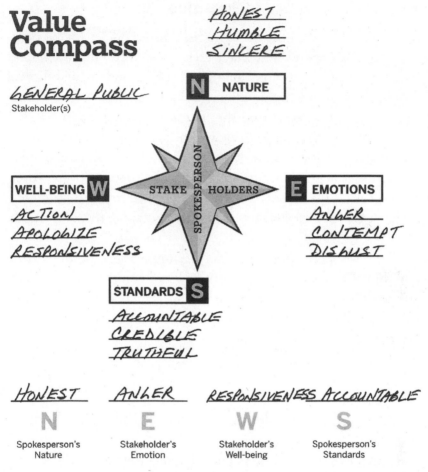

Value Compass

HONEST
HUMBLE
SINCERE

GENERAL PUBLIC
Stakeholder(s)

N NATURE

STAKE SPOKESPERSON HOLDERS

WELL-BEING **W**
ACTION
APOLOGIZE
RESPONSIVENESS

E EMOTIONS
ANGER
CONTEMPT
DISGUST

STANDARDS **S**
ACCOUNTABLE
CREDIBLE
TRUTHFUL

HONEST	ANGER	RESPONSIVENESS	ACCOUNTABLE
N	E	W	S
Spokesperson's Nature	Stakeholder's Emotion	Stakeholder's Well-being	Spokesperson's Standards

© Jeff Ansell 2010

Now the client can filter future messages through the four chosen Value Compass words to ensure media messages match organizational values. Is the message *honest*? Does it acknowledge the general public's *anger*? Is it *responsive* to stakeholders' needs? Does it reflect the organization's *accountability*? If so, then the client knows those organizational messages will help build stakeholder confidence and trust.

Biojax Part 2: The Value Compass in Practice

Remember Joan Smith, the chief executive officer for biopharmaceutical company JLA Life Sciences? As we saw in Chapter One, she was questioned about the price and availability of Biojax, a new and highly effective biological drug for treating cancer. Joan was convinced she had a positive story to tell, but she discovered that an interview can quickly turn antagonistic. Fortunately for Joan, she will get another chance in Chapter Six to address concerns surrounding Biojax. To prepare for her interview do-over, Joan needs to create a Value Compass. During one of our sessions, I sat down with Joan to help her through the six steps just outlined.

First, we spent some time identifying her stakeholders. For a new biological therapy, her stakeholders could be the general public or doctors or health care payers. They could be patients, their families, or activist groups. To narrow down the options, I asked her who was most affected by the price and availability of Biojax.

"Patients," she said.

"Why patients?" I asked.

"They're the ones with the most at stake. They're fighting for their lives."

"True, but are they the group you most hope to reach through the interview?"

"I don't know. I hope to reach everyone."

"No, I mean if you had to pick one group you hope will read the story, would it be patients?"

She thought about it, then nodded. "Yes, absolutely. Patients are the ones who need to mobilize and help pressure the government and insurance companies to add Biojax to their reimbursement list."

With that settled, we focused on the spokesperson axis. Starting with (N)ature, Joan read through the Value Compass words list. After a few stops and starts, she chose *concerned*, *empathetic*, and *honest*.

I asked her why she chose those three words.

She said the impression she had was that people felt JLA Life Sciences was callous and deceptive in its pricing practices. "People don't understand the costs and challenges in bringing a new drug to market," she explained. "We're being honest and up-front about those costs. People made a lot of sacrifices and they deserve to be rewarded. But that doesn't mean we don't appreciate the feelings of patients. We do. We're concerned about patients and we understand the difficulties they face."

Next, Joan read through the possible words for (S)tandards. The terms that stood out to her were *credible, ethical,* and *trustworthy*. She felt these three words represented corporate standards that countered the impression that JLA Life Sciences was dishonest and heartless. "We really are trying to do the right thing," she said. "We're trying to help people live longer, better lives."

With the spokesperson axis complete, we shifted to the stakeholders axis. I asked what emotions her stakeholders might feel while listening to a discussion about the price and availability of Biojax. "In other words," I said, "if you were a cancer patient, how would you feel?"

"I'd be angry."

"Why?"

"Because here's this product that can help me, that's proven to lengthen lives, but I can't get it."

"What else?"

"I'd be disgusted. I mean, this looks like another case of corporate greed. And I guess I'd be worried, too."

"Worried about what?"

"About my future. About my family and how long I have to live."

"Those are all very strong emotions."

"No kidding," Joan said grimly. After she filled in the three lines for (E)motions, we moved to the stakeholders' (W)ell-being. I asked her what she thought JLA Life Sciences could do to enhance the well-being of people who are angry, disgusted, and worried.

"Be responsive," she replied almost immediately. "Patients need to know we're listening. That we care."

"And?"

"And—" She scanned through the list of words.

"Let me put it another way," I said. "These are people fighting for their lives, right?"

"Yes, absolutely."

"To help with that fight, what do they most need?"

"Biojax," Joan said. "But we can't just give it away."

"Then how can patients get it?"

Joan's face brightened. "By getting involved. They need to write their representatives. They need to join cancer activist groups and put pressure on the government and insurance companies to pay for Biojax."

"Can you help them do those things?" I asked.

"Sure, I guess."

"How?"

"I see where this is going," Joan said, smiling. "We can help by educating patients. By telling them who to contact and providing the information they need to leverage decision makers." She filled in the remaining blanks on the stakeholder axis. This may seem like a somewhat involved process, but it actually took less than five minutes. Figure 2.3 shows how Joan's Value Compass looked at this point.

Now it was time to choose one word from each category. Often, this seems like the hardest part. As Joan said at the time: "They all look like good words."

I told her not to worry. It's actually easier than it appears. "Let's just take a few minutes to work through each category," I suggested.

Figure 2.3 Partial Biojax Value Compass

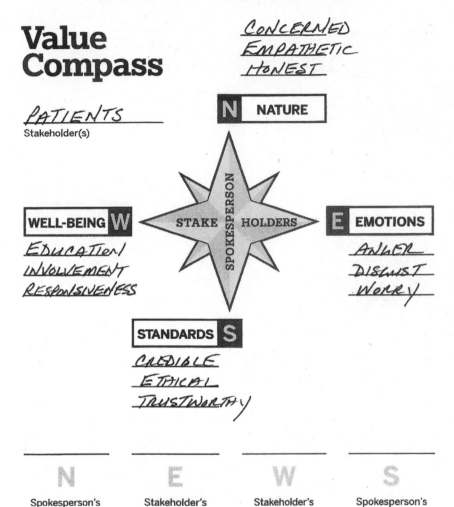

We started with (N)ature. Although it was important to be honest and concerned, Joan decided it was most important to appear empathetic. "If we're empathetic, if we make it clear we understand their challenges and fears, then patients will know JLA Life Sciences is on their side."

Figure 2.4 Final Biojax Value Compass

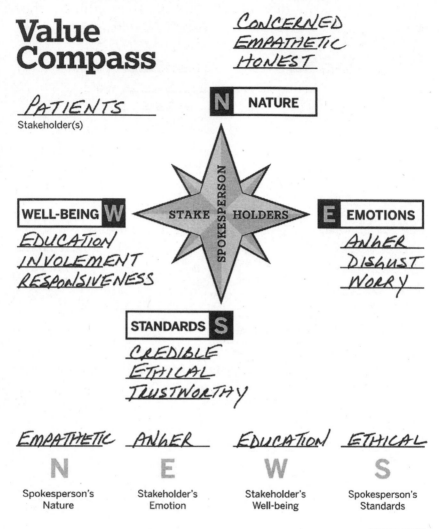

The (E)motions category was even easier. "More than anything, patients are angry," Joan said. "They feel powerless. They feel like they're being taken advantage of or sacrificed."

When we moved to (W)ell-being, Joan said, "I guess I've already figured this one out. Patients need to get involved. They need to begin changing policy."

"But—" I started to say.

"I know," Joan interrupted. "To do those things, they need education." She wrote education in the blank line above "W."

Last, we addressed (S)tandards. Joan carefully considered the three options. "When profits and medicine are mixed," she said, "it's always an issue of ethics. People are questioning our motives. It's important that we make it clear to patients that above all else, we're ethical."

With a clear understanding of how she wants her organization to be perceived and valuable insight into her stakeholders' perspective, Joan is now ready to begin addressing her critics. Joan's final Value Compass is presented in Figure 2.4.

When people mired in bad news are asked to identify the words in their Value Compass, the same terms are often used. Predictably, most people say they want to be seen as sincere, honest, credible, and competent. What separates people and organizations, however, is not the words they choose to describe their values but rather how they express and implement those values. The next few chapters provide specific tools and strategies for transforming your chosen values into messages that convert words into commitments and commitments into action.

Chapter Talking Points

- When a reporter makes contact, follow these three steps: be friendly, create a buffer zone, and ask questions to determine her or his intentions.
- When talking to a reporter, be careful of what you say and remember there's no such thing as "off the record." When in doubt, leave it out.
- To better manage your image, follow what others are saying about your company or organization in the media, on the Web, and in blogs.

- Be aware of how you come across. There's no benefit to being seen as defensive, argumentative, or unresponsive. Instead, project an image of openness, honesty, and empathy.

- To project a positive image, first ask yourself, "What's the right thing to do?"

- To ensure that you're doing the right thing, look to your values. The Value Compass is an effective tool for establishing and focusing your values, particularly when public trust is threatened.

3

HOW TO ADMIT BAD NEWS

"Sunlight is the best disinfectant."
—*U.S. Supreme Court Justice Louis Brandeis*

When the news isn't good, spokespeople must be front-and-center to tell their story before others start telling it for them. Robert Dilenschneider, former boss of PR firm Hill and Knowlton, used to say that when the news is bad, "tell it all and tell it fast." But in shaping and telling their story, spokespeople need a pathway that builds on their Value Compass so that their messages reflect the attributes they hope to project. This chapter will focus on the importance of being present and responsive when bad news happens, as well as explain the four key principles for building trust. It will also provide a simple yet powerful formula for crafting bad news messages that reflect Value Compass results and can withstand even the most ruthless media edit.

Bad News Basics

When bad news happens, people have a tendency to either withdraw from the media or trivialize the situation. When the emergency department at Sunrise Hospital in New York was accused of turning away an uninsured homeless man with chest pain who died moments later, the hospital's spokesperson was asked by ABC News to comment. "We're all going to die," the spokesperson said. True, but not really an appropriate comment considering the circumstance. In the aftermath of the 2009 earthquake in Italy that killed 260 people and left 18,000 homeless, Italian Prime Minister Silvio Berlusconi told survivors to consider themselves on a camping weekend. "Go to the beach," said Berlusconi. "Take a short vacation." Thanks for your concern, Prime Minister. To avoid coming across as insensitive or glib, there are three fundamental concepts you should keep in mind in order to present yourself and your organization in a positive manner.

Be Accessible and Forthcoming

Lying low is rarely a good strategy when it comes to dealing with reporters who are searching for comments or answers. Failing to make oneself available to media when problems arise only yields the floor to others who will speak, and what they say will no doubt be critical. As an old public relations adage goes, "Mess up, 'fess up." Within days of taking over from Eliot Spitzer as New York governor, David Patterson held a news conference to admit infidelity by both him and his wife. "I didn't want to be compromised," he explained. "I didn't want to be blackmailed. I didn't want to hesitate taking an action because a person on the other side might hurt me or my family."

In covering tragic or distressing stories, reporters look to put a human face on those affected or harmed by the negative event. Putting a face on a story humanizes it, making it much more personal and emotionally charged. Too often, however, companies or organizations accused of perpetrating the wrong remain faceless. If they offer comments at all, it is frequently in the form of a news release or prepared statement, rather than a heartfelt message delivered by a human being. These kinds of approaches leave members of the public believing that a company responsible for or associated with a major problem is unwilling to take ownership of it.

I'm not suggesting that just showing up and saying something is enough to mitigate damage. Telling a reporter "no comment" can be nearly as detrimental as not saying anything during a PR crisis. Anyone who believes bad news stories go away when companies refuse to talk to the media is presumably watching *SpongeBob SquarePants* while *Dateline* is on. A self-incriminating quote that implies you know something and choose not to answer, "no comment" is generally uttered by guilty people with a bead of sweat slowly trickling down their forehead. It is a hackneyed phrase that only serves to reinforce distrust and make a story appear more ominous and compelling. As such, a "no comment" response extends the news cycle of a negative story at a time when a spokesperson's objective should be to shorten it.

An example of the damage a "no comment" response can cause occurred after an August 1993 explosion at the Alusuisse Flexible Packaging plant in Shelbyville, Kentucky. The explosion killed a nineteen-year-old student named Paul Brierly. Local reporters converged on the plant looking for comment, but Alusuisse refused to speak to the media. When a company official finally decided to comment, what he said left a lot to be desired: "My name is Phil Sheppard. I am safety director of Alusuisse. The comment we have at this time is that we will not have any comment until ten o'clock tomorrow morning." That evening, the local news reported the company had "no comment." Sheppard's lack of message spoke volumes and was indeed a message in itself, devoid of fact or feeling. This solidified the community's impression of a company on the run. By the time Alusuisse did choose to say more, the tragedy, as well as the company's presumed guilt, had become a nationwide story on network newscasts and in major-market newspapers.

Three Points to Remember in Tragic Situations

Communicating with the media in tragic circumstances requires messages that are appropriately worded and strike the correct tone. For example, consider the following statement: "At nine A.M. today, we had an unfortunate incident in our facility involving a worker who was killed near the scene of an explosion. We are currently conducting a detailed investigation regarding the cause of the explosion. We will update you as soon as we have a further understanding of the cause." Although this statement may be true and the information accurate, the spokesperson should have kept three points in mind when addressing this tragic event:

- **Avoid calling a death an "incident."** The word "incident" trivializes a fatality. The death of a person is tragic and the language spokespeople use must reflect that.
- **Invoke the credibility offered by third parties.** Critics will question the integrity of your investigation, so highlight the role of a credible third party in determining the cause. In plant accidents, a probe led by the Occupational Health and Safety Administration (OSHA) is seen as more transparent.
- **You are not the only source for information.** Corporate spokespeople may mistakenly believe that reporters are reliant solely on them for information in a crisis. The media get their information from many credible sources, including fire and EMT officials, OSHA, and other employees.

Alusuisse's delayed response and the ensuing media attention led to a coroner's inquest, followed by a criminal investigation and lawsuit, all of which caused long-term damage to Alusuisse's business and reputation. A teenager's death is always a heart-rending tragedy, and Alusuisse failed to comprehend the interest it would attract or the intensity of emotion it would unleash. That's why it is critical for spokespeople not only to understand the emotions triggered by a negative news event but also to acknowledge those emotions publicly.

Be Among Those Most Upset

When bad news happens, you have to be among those most upset about the situation, even if your negligence caused it. Media and other stakeholders will look to you to see your reaction. Are you responding with genuine concern? Or, is there a callous or indifferent manner to the delivery of your message? Your response must reflect compassion and empathy, both in content and tone. In addition to saying the right words, you must look as if you genuinely believe what you're saying. In some cases, you will be handed messages crafted by others. Then your challenge is to convey those messages in a real and authentic way. Being among those most upset demonstrates your sincerity in acknowledging a damaging situation and reflects an appreciation of the impact that situation has on stakeholders. When bad news happens, people don't care how much you know, they need to know how much you care.

There is often reluctance, however, to express regret or remorse, especially in situations where litigation is either possible or actually unfolding. By being among those most upset, some people are concerned they give credence to the claims made by those who have either been wronged or feel wronged. "I believe that it actually has the opposite effect," says lawyer Jim Golden, whose clients have been responsible for accidents leading to fatalities. "The premium value on claims comes in when you refuse to step up and admit the truth as opposed to the reverse." Golden believes expressing regret and empathy facilitates mutually beneficial outcomes. David Parker, the CEO of Covenant Transportation Group, one of the largest truckload carriers in the United States, agrees: "Because of this empathetic, proactive approach, our claims costs have been reduced by millions of dollars." Parker also believes his company has benefited in its relationship with its insurance carrier. "This approach contributed directly to a $1,000,000 insurance premium rebate we recently received," says Parker. Likewise, Mark Whitehead, VP of Claims and Litigation for trucking giant JB Hunt, estimates that an empathetic approach has created savings of 15 to 30 percent in catastrophic personal injury claims. In most cases, these types of reductions in claims costs translate directly to a company's bottom line.[1]

Know That Facts Will Never Win Over Emotion

Historically, public relations professionals bombarded people with facts and figures designed to persuade them that there was no reason to worry about company performance, the new dump-site, or the proposed low-cost housing project. Corporate executives and spokespeople traditionally talked over and around the emotional concerns of others, not fully realizing the alienating nature of that approach. The fact is that news is about emotion.

At the MIT–Harvard program "Dealing with an Angry Public," which I deliver with Larry Susskind and Mike Wheeler, attendees often tell us they take the course to learn how to get emotional people to focus only on facts. Hearing that makes us chuckle. Spokespeople, especially those schooled in engineering, science, and technology, rely on the recitation of facts to persuade people of the rightness of their cause. Facts, after all, speak for themselves. But facts used to counter emotion are not enough to convince people who are upset or distraught. For them, facts are incidental. All the facts in the world may prove a point, but if individuals feel strongly about an issue they'll go with their gut.

Consider the case of Olestra, a food additive created by Procter & Gamble that lowered or eliminated fat content in snack foods. Approved by the U.S. Food and Drug Administration (FDA) in 1996, it was released with the warning that "Olestra may cause abdominal cramping and loose stools." Even though the condition only occurred in a small number of cases and due to excessive consumption, the general public became alarmed at the prospect of losing control in a humiliating way. The wide-spread use of terms like "anal leakage" only increased the fear of embarrassment. In response, Procter & Gamble worked to high-light the statistical safety and positive attributes of Olestra. Procter & Gamble's spokespeople pointed out that over five billion servings of Olestra-infused products had safely been eaten by consumers. They referenced the hundreds of clinical tests that validated Olestra's safety. They explained that since Olestra's initial approval, the FDA had reviewed the food additive three additional times, including an extensive post-marketing study that led to the removal of the "loose stool" warning. But no matter how many studies or statistics Procter & Gamble provided, it couldn't overcome the cultural condemnation created by people's fear of humiliation. By 2002, Procter & Gamble gave up on Olestra as a food additive and sold its factory in Cincinnati.

Because facts and numbers can never win over emotion, spokespeople tasked with communicating bad news need to identify the underlying emotions felt by the people directly affected. Are they angry? Frightened? Worried? To help empathize with stakeholders, imagine the iceberg of emotion that lies beneath your issue. For instance, if you're in the utility business and part of your power grid goes down, customers will feel frustrated and angry. Even if it's just one block in a grid that serves miles of households and businesses, the affected customers will be without lights and cut off from news and information outlets. They may lose important data and perishable food. Likewise, if your factory mistakenly ships a tainted product, consumers will be suspicious of your processes. Even if your quality control rate is 99.99 percent, if a single child or pet is hurt by your mistake the damage will be considerable. The ensuing feelings of outrage and grief will be reported, not your 99.99 percent quality-control rate. Therefore, instead of regurgitating facts and figures, focus on the emotions that underpin the issues you and your organization face. The Value Compass, explained in Chapter Two, is a particularly helpful tool for identifying the primary emotions of stakeholders and victims.

Providing Reasons to Trust

Trust is not something you can simply tell people to have. Trust is something that must be earned. And when that earned trust is violated, people must be provided with reasons to once again believe you, presuming they ever did in the first place. When a spokesperson tells people, "Trust me," it actually has the opposite effect. Instead of encouraging trust or confidence, it sends off a smarmy signal that puts people on high alert. They then filter what they hear through a prism of distrust.

The Two Types of Trust Violations

According to a Washington University research study, there are two types of trust violations. The first type involves a breach of integrity, with examples being a world-class athlete accused of steroid use or a politician embroiled in a sex scandal. The second type of trust violation is based on competency and reflects on the abilities and knowledge of an individual or organization. Widespread delays in the airline industry or medical malpractice cases are examples of competency violations.

In a study entitled *Silence Speaks Volumes*, researchers examined how people respond to both types of trust violations. Disturbingly, the research discovered that the best approach to dealing with integrity-based violations is to deny the allegation, rather than apologize for what happened. "Apologizing for it and owning up to it can have some negative effects," said Professor Kurt Dirks, one of the study's coauthors. "Once you're branded as a liar or thief you can't come back from that." On the other hand, the study confirmed that people respond positively to apologies for competence-based violations. "Apologize, very clearly," recommended Professor Dirks. "Apologize and provide a reason why this is not going to happen again."[2]

Spokespeople also chip away at trust when they simply regurgitate messages that are designed to make them look good even though a situation may be damaging or tragic. To help build trust and ensure that comments are not interpreted as dishonest or dismissive, follow these four guiding principles:

- Show humility.
- Answer honestly.
- Acknowledge skepticism.
- Couple concern with commitment to action.

To ensure you stay on the course charted by your Value Compass, use these four principles as guideposts during a media interaction or public relations crisis.

Show Humility

Communicating with confidence is important. The secret, though, is in knowing when to convey confidence, when to convey humility, and how to hold each in perfect balance. Confidence without humility is perceived as cockiness, while humility without confidence is perceived as weakness. In counseling and coaching corporate and government leaders, I emphasize the importance of communicating with humility. I tell clients the richer and more powerful they are, the more they need to be humble. Otherwise, the media will pounce on any opportunity to disgrace them.

Take the case of publishing mogul Conrad Black, whose empire spanned more than five hundred newspapers, including the prestigious London *Telegraph* and the popular *Chicago Sun-Times*. On trial for fraud and obstructing justice, Black, who owned four luxurious homes and two dozen cars, asserted that a typical Chicago jury member who "does not reside in more than one residence, employ servants or a chauffeur, enjoy lavish furniture, or host expensive parties" should not be considered one of his peers.[3] Of shareholders upset about his excessive compensation, Black said, "I would like to just blow their asses off."[4] He even told audit committee members he would "hose down" investors unhappy about the millions of dollars in fees he paid himself. "My advice to Mr. Black was to be a little more humble," said Marie-Josée Kravis, a former member of his company's audit committee.[5]

U.S. sentencing guidelines allow judges the latitude to go easier on defendants who show contrition or are generally of good character. In hopes of mustering empathy for Black, his friends launched a campaign to spread the message that he is gracious and humble to all he meets. "Conrad Black is a person with a deep reservoir of kindness and generosity consistently exhibited to people of all stations in life," his friends claimed in a court document.[6] But it made no difference. Attempts to build empathy for Black were too little, too late. He was sentenced to six and a half years in a Florida prison.

Answer Honestly

When executives and spokespeople shy away from being honest, the truth has a way of catching up with them. Not being honest or not coming across as honest makes a spokesperson look and sound evasive and untrustworthy. This is not to suggest that a media interview needs to be a confessional. Certainly, there are some questions that for a variety of legal or ethical reasons cannot or should not be answered. Those include questions pertaining to privileged or confidential information. Yet there is a difference between having a good reason not to answer honestly and attempting to mislead people. Balancing this need to be honest while not saying something harmful can be like walking the thin edge of a razor: it is easy to teeter. In my experience, though, it is always better to teeter toward the side of honesty.

For instance, when retail sales are weak, most store executives choose to blame the economy, job losses, or cyclical spending rather than their own strategies. Yet Mona Williams, vice president of communications for Wal-Mart, responded truthfully when the retailer's strategy of offering less aggressive discounts led to a drop in sales. Williams said, "We are disappointed with our sales performance for the Friday after Thanksgiving and the full weekend." With hindsight she said, "Our overall program was too predictable and our competition capitalized on this."[7] Williams's candor no doubt surprised reporters who expected her to toot Wal-Mart's horn about size, scope, and value. Predictably, the stock price took an immediate hit. But because Wal-Mart was honest with both itself and the public, sales rebounded within the next twelve months. Today, Wal-Mart is viewed by investors as one of the strongest companies in the discount and variety store sector.

In contrast, following the coming together of Chrysler and Daimler, Jurgen Shrempp, chairman of the German company, claimed the alliance of the two automakers was a merger of equals, not a takeover. The statement turned out to be bogus. It was definitely a takeover, as Chrysler's leadership team was largely pushed aside so the Daimler people could run the business. Asked later why he lied, Shrempp said he chose to be "misleading" for "psychological" reasons.[8] Shrempp's mistruth triggered legal action in the courts, with investors saying material information was withheld. In the end, Daimler was forced to sell Chrysler in 2007 to a private equity firm for $650 million, a 98 percent discount from the $36 billion Daimler originally paid in 1998.

While the two preceding examples are deliberately clear-cut, the fact is that honesty can be viewed as existing on a continuum. On one end of the continuum is the absolute "tell the truth" and on the other end is "don't lie." For spokespeople dealing with sensitive matters, there is significant maneuvering room between these two extremes. Consequently, they must be able to negotiate this continuum, especially when much is at stake. For example, in the later stages of the U.S. Civil War, President Abraham Lincoln did not want reporters to find out that Confederate representatives were en route to talk peace. Asked whether the southerners were indeed in the U.S. capital, Lincoln, who knew they were en route to Fort Monroe, Virginia, responded, "So far as I know, there are no Peace Commissioners in the city, or likely to be in it." President Lincoln was in fact answering honestly based on the way the question was asked. He did not lie, though clearly his answer was intended to mislead. Doing so, however, helped bring the Civil War to a quicker end.[9]

Acknowledge Skepticism

Admitting that some people may feel skeptical about an issue or situation can be difficult for a spokesperson. Once again, the fear is that by acknowledging the doubts that others express, those concerns are being legitimized. But sometimes people need to hear a spokesperson acknowledge that stakeholders are unconvinced by a specific claim. Doing so actually helps enhance credibility.

Too often, however, spokespeople who comment on problems they would rather not address rely on traditional media response strategies that focus mostly on benefits and positive messages. Students at Toronto's York University were traumatized by the rape of two women in their campus dormitory. "I'm scared to go to the bathroom myself," said the two women's neighbor, nineteen-year-old student Houry Seukunian. "We go (to the bathroom) in packs now," Seukunian told the *Toronto Star*. "I knew our campus wasn't safe." Commenting on the dorm attacks, a university spokesman defended security at the school. "Our dormitories are safe," he stated unequivocally.[10] Two young women were raped in the dormitory and the spokesman says the dorm is safe? As a parent myself, I can't help but feel that the spokesman's quote is dismissive and fails to acknowledge the anxiety of both students and parents. Instead, the spokesman should have said, "Though we do all we can to keep our dormitories safe, we'll work with police and students to see how we can keep terrible events like this from taking place."

Too Evil to Trust

What to do if a corporation within a vilified industry wants to acknowledge people's skepticism, yet people don't believe any of its messages? Sectors that fall into this category include the nuclear industry, weapons manufacturers, and tobacco companies. Considering the predisposition not to believe what spokespeople for these sectors say, it is an uphill battle for them to acknowledge skepticism. British American Tobacco (BAT) wanted to give it a try after it launched a corporate social responsibility program. BAT invited antismoking groups to come to meetings facilitated by a neutral third party. Not surprisingly, most people viewed the initiative as a meaningless exercise in public relations and refused to participate. Only four of the twenty-four U.K. medical groups invited came to the first meeting. Acknowledging the public's response, a BAT executive said, "We have been under such attack from pressure groups and regulators that we felt trying to have a rational debate was futile. We needed to demonstrate a different approach." Was it enough to simply acknowledge a fuming public's skepticism? No. But you have to buy a lottery ticket to win. An angry public may loathe the product a company sells, but they cannot fault it for being willing to engage with those who want them shut down.

Acknowledging skepticism can go a long way toward enhancing credibility and assuring people that their concerns are being taken seriously. When shareholders weren't buying into the supposed merits of a merger between brewing giants Molson and Coors, Molson CEO Dan O'Neill knew his messages about improved profit margins and shareholder value weren't resonating. The proposed merger looked doomed until O'Neill admitted to the *Globe and Mail* business section that Molson had not done a good job of selling shareholders on the deal. "I think the overall feeling that we have is there's still a lot of skepticism," said O'Neill.[11] Although it may have seemed that he was admitting defeat, shareholders later voted to approve the Molson-Coors merger.

Admitting there is skepticism can sometimes involve the acknowledgment of a painful truth. In the wake of sex scandals involving the Catholic Church, some of their spokespeople went so far as to blame their youthful victims. Realizing this approach of denial and attack was doing the Church great harm, Father James Flavin of Boston took it upon himself to act as a voice for those clergy outraged by what had been allowed to happen. Father Flavin told *Newsweek* magazine, "I wouldn't trust other priests right now, either."[12] Father Flavin's quote acknowledged what everyone already knew to be true and acted as a first step in the long process of atonement.

Couple Concern with Commitment to Action

In bad news situations, it is not nearly enough to express concern; there must be action taken to confront the problem. Concern without action is meaningless rhetoric. Consider the story of six BP Amoco scientists in Naperville, Illinois, who developed the same rare form of brain cancer. The scientists worked in what became known as "the cancer building." To investigate, BP Amoco brought in medical experts to confirm what role, if any, the company played in causing the cancer cluster. At a news conference to share its findings, BP Amoco confirmed it was the cause of the problem and made three announcements. It closed the lab in the "cancer building." It offered free MRIs for anyone who ever worked in the building. It hired medical experts to review seventeen hundred medical records. Lawyers will argue that without evidence plaintiffs may not be able to bring a case forward, let alone prove it in court, but BP Amoco chose a different path. Of the six scientists, five of the families settled with the company.

However, there may be some situations in which people are worried about health impacts even though there is no concrete evidence that a problem exists. In this case, a company should acknowledge the concerns that people have, but is it obliged to take action? Picture a crowded town hall meeting, the type that takes place in a high school auditorium or church basement. A local developer is on hand getting an earful from townsfolk worried about chemical contamination at the old battery plant site, where an office building is planned. The site is adjacent to a park where children play ball, and until state environment officials confirm the chemicals pose no problem, the community remains unconvinced. A microphone is passed to a mother who stands and asks the developer, "What if there are dangerous chemicals buried at the site? What are you going to do to keep our kids safe until we know for sure?"

Thinking quickly, the developer remembers that a media trainer once told him never to answer speculative questions. So, he tells the mother, "It's inappropriate to speculate on what's in the ground," adding "the community is not in danger." People then grow angry because the developer is not listening to their safety concerns, which makes perfect fodder for reporters in attendance. So far, the incident has loads of conflict, driven by outraged residents and a defensive developer. It's shaping up to be a classic good-versus-evil narrative—and a front page story.

What is actually required of the developer is an answer that captures the emotion of the moment coupled with an action step that will satisfy the upset community. Once again, the mother's primary question is, "What are you going to do to keep our kids safe until we know for sure?" Remembering his Value Compass, the developer now says, "It's very clear the community has important concerns about the property, so until everyone knows for certain we will build a fence to keep people off the site." The developer's response is empathetic and conciliatory. More importantly, it doesn't merely articulate the community's concerns, it

Wrongly Accused

What if a company is wrongly accused? Dina is the chief medical officer for a brand-name pharmaceutical company. During clinical trials for a new antidepressant, two patients mysteriously died. Dina believes the deaths are unrelated to testing, yet authorities suspect negligence. The challenge for Dina is to find a way to acknowledge the patient deaths while not taking the blame for them prematurely. It is a tricky message to deliver, for fear of sounding defensive. Dina's statement should be, "What happened was very sad and though we followed each and every safety procedure, we're determined to help authorities answer every single question." This response acknowledges the patients' deaths and emphasizes that safety protocols were respected. Further, it conveys her desire to ensure the truth is known.

promises action that will provide a solution to their immediate needs.

The Problem Solution Formula

As previously mentioned, the reporter's quest is for conflict, not solutions. Conflict pays for the kids' braces and sends them to camp in the summer, which is why reporters instinctively zero in on inflammatory, defensive-sounding quotes. In situations where there are problems reported and also solutions provided, reporters will still tend to highlight the problems, in some cases treating the solution as an afterthought. Therefore, spokespeople need a formula or strategy that allows them to honestly address a problem while at the same time ensuring that the solution will be quoted. The Problem Solution Formula helps do that.

As the name implies, the Problem Solution Formula is a structured response that joins the problem and solution in one sentence. It is generally made up of two clauses or phrases joined by a conjunction. The first clause or phrase identifies and frames the problem; the second clause or phrase offers a solution to that problem. By combining the two components in one sentence, the statement is much more likely to survive the media editing process intact. To optimize the Problem Solution Formula, the message should be filtered through the Value Compass to ensure that it reflects how you and your company want to be perceived. Following are three examples of how to construct a basic Problem Solution Formula message:

1. Three workers at a courier company sorting facility contracted the H1N1 virus, leaving two employees dead and a third in critical condition.

Problem: H1N1 flu virus has killed two employees and put a third in critical condition.
Solution: Close the facility and bring in health officials to test all workers and determine the source of the H1N1 virus.
Problem Solution Formula message: Sadly, the virus has claimed the lives of two of our colleagues and has placed a third in critical condition, so we have closed the facility while state health officials test all workers and determine the source of the virus.

This message acknowledges the severity of the problem and recognizes the government's responsibility to investigate and manage this growing public health issue.

2. A pet food company has been accused of selling contaminated food products. The products are responsible for making hundreds of dogs and cats ill.

Problem: Pets and their owners have been terribly affected.
Solution: Recall tainted products from stores.
Problem Solution Formula message: We're sorry that pets and their owners have been terribly affected and we have voluntarily recalled all products on store shelves.

This message acknowledges the suffering of pets and their owners and makes a commitment to remove the harmful product from circulation.

3. A software company has just sent out a software update that caused millions of computers to crash.

Problem: People have been inconvenienced.
Solution: Provide support and product replacement.
Problem Solution Formula message: We apologize to everyone inconvenienced by our mistake and we are now offering support plus free product replacement.

This message acknowledges customers' frustration and offers them a means to resolve any problems created by the faulty software update.

These brief examples outline the basics of how to compose a Problem Solution Formula message, but keep in mind that certain situations call for messages to be directed at different audiences. If a company was laying off a significant portion of its workforce, for instance, the following message would be aimed at the mainstream media: "Regrettably, two hundred workers will be laid off and we'll do our best to ensure they have a smooth transition." For a business audience, the appropriate message would read, "We needed to take this action to keep the company strong and we'll now assist the affected employees while we consolidate our operations."

You can find a template for crafting your own Problem Solution Formula messages in the Appendix. This helpful template provides all the instruction and guidance needed to create an effective, meaningful response during a bad news situation. The following step-by-step, in-depth example illustrates how to use this template. It will also help you begin the process of implementing the Value Compass and the Problem Solution Formula in real-world situations.

Biojax Part 3: The Problem Solution Formula in Practice

In Chapter One, Joan Smith, chief executive officer of JLA Life Sciences Corporation, was repeatedly asked by a reporter why her company's new biologic drug, Biojax, is so expensive. The persistent questioning rattled Joan and as a result, she responded in a curt, argumentative manner. The resulting news story had Joan and her company coming across as uncaring and greedy. Joan wanted another opportunity to answer the question of why Biojax is priced higher than more traditional therapies.

In deciding how to compose an answer, Joan wanted to make three main points. First, she wanted people to appreciate the unique science behind Biojax, so they would see the merits of reimbursement. Second, in a conciliatory way, Joan wanted to remind government about its role in this debate. Third, Joan wanted her statement to include a message about people with cancer. Here is what she came up with: "Because the anticancer activity in Biojax is attributed to the general microtubule destabilizing properties of certain alkaloids, the expenditure to research, develop, and manufacture the compound was prohibitive. Currently, we are engaged in dialogue with government as well as various payer groups to determine whether reimbursement is forthcoming. Reimbursements to cancer victims will allow them access to the medication."

Technically, Joan's words in the answer are accurate; however, the three points she hoped to make are lost. Let's review the answer sentence by sentence. "Because the anticancer activity in Biojax is attributed to the general microtubule destabilizing properties of certain alkaloids, the expenditure to research, develop, and manufacture the compound was prohibitive." This sentence presents a challenge to the journalist because it is difficult to understand and not particularly quotable.

The second sentence in Joan's answer reads, "Currently, we are engaged in dialogue with government as well as various payer groups to determine whether reimbursement is forthcoming." This sentence is officious-sounding and bureaucratic. Also, it makes it seem as if JLA Life Sciences is primarily concerned with collecting money.

Her third sentence reads, "Reimbursements to cancer victims will allow them access to the medication." Yes, the message is about people with cancer, only her use of the word "victims" is depersonalizing. The fact is none of these quotes would look good in print or help alter the perception of JLA Life Sciences as uncaring and greedy.

While Joan made a few missteps in formulating her statement, her first mistake was not referring to her Value Compass. As a reminder, Joan's stakeholders are "patients" and her four Value Compass words are "empathetic," "anger," "education," and "ethical." If you would like to see Joan's Value Compass or review the process for determining Value Compass words, refer to the end of Chapter Two.

To help create a new, more effective response, Joan turned to the Problem Solution Formula template that can be found in the Appendix. She started by filling in the "stakeholders" blank and transferring her four Value Compass terms to the appropriate spaces. Before she started on the next step, I reminded her to use language appropriate for her stakeholders. "Remember," I told her, "patients aren't scientists, doctors, or regulatory employees."

Joan nodded and moved on to determining the two separate clauses and creating her Problem Solution Formula message.

Problem: Biojax is expensive due to the high cost of manufacturing medicine made from living cells.
Solution: Government needs to help people battling cancer by offering coverage for this important medicine.
Problem Solution Formula message: Unfortunately, Biojax is expensive due to the high cost of manufacturing medicine made

from living cells, so government needs to help people battling cancer by offering coverage for this important medicine.

Structurally, note that the entire response is captured in one sentence. The first half of the sentence frames the problem (Biojax is expensive due to its science), while the second half of the sentence addresses the solution (government needs to cover its cost). But does Joan's new message address the three primary points she hoped to make? Yes, it clearly and plainly identifies the science behind Biojax, reminds government of its role in the debate, and includes a message about people with cancer. Is Joan's new message reflective of her Value Compass? Terms like "unfortunately" and "battling cancer" indicate empathy with a cancer patient's plight. "Battling" also touches on patient anger by recognizing the frustration and struggle cancer patients face while literally fighting for their lives. By mentioning the science behind Biojax and pointing out that government determines its availability, the statement educates patients. Finally, by offering an honest explanation for why Biojax is more expensive than other treatments, the statement reinforces a perception of ethical behavior. Now consider Joan's new response in the context of an interview:

> *Interviewer*: Why is Biojax so expensive?
> *Joan Smith*: Unfortunately, Biojax is expensive due to the high cost of manufacturing medicine made from living cells, so government needs to help people battling cancer by offering coverage for this important medicine.

Joan's new message is still accurate and honest. But this time around, it's also quotable. As for which quote the reporter will use, there are three editing options:

- The entire answer (most likely option): "Unfortunately, Biojax is expensive due to the high cost of manufacturing medicine made from living cells, so government needs to help people battling cancer by offering coverage for this important medicine."

- The first portion of the answer: "Unfortunately, Biojax is expensive due to the high cost of manufacturing medicine made from living cells."
- The last portion of the answer: "Government needs to help people battling cancer by offering coverage for this important medicine."

Regardless of the quote selected, all match Joan's Value Compass and present JLA Life Sciences in a positive light. With an effective Problem Solution Formula message in hand, the next step for Joan is to start developing a full range of compelling messages to use in her upcoming media interview.

Chapter Talking Points

- To avoid looking insensitive or glib when bad news happens, remember these three fundamental concepts: be accessible, be among those most upset, and know that facts will never win over emotion.
- In order to stay on the appropriate path during a PR crisis, it is beneficial to follow the four principles for building trust:
  - Show humility.
  - Answer honestly.
  - Acknowledge skepticism.
  - Couple concern with commitment to action.
- Reporters tend to emphasize problems and obscure solutions. The Problem Solution Formula allows you to address a problem honestly while simultaneously ensuring that the solution will be quoted.

- The Problem Solution Formula is a structured response made up of two clauses or phrases joined by a conjunction. The first clause or phrase identifies and frames the problem while the second clause or phrase offers a solution to that problem.

- To optimize Problem Solution Formula messages, filter them through the Value Compass to ensure they reflect the values you and your organization want to present to the public.

4

CRAFTING COMPELLING
MESSAGES

"Say all you have to say in the fewest possible
words, or your reader will be sure to skip them;
and in the plainest possible words, or he will
certainly misunderstand them."

—*John Ruskin, Victorian writer and critic*

A fascinating study published in the *Journal of Personality and Social Psychology* found that repeated exposure to one person's perspective and viewpoint has almost as much influence as exposure to shared opinions from many people. The lead author of the study, Kimberlee Weaver of Virginia Polytechnic Institute and State University, discovered that "feelings of familiarity increase with the number of exposures, independent of their source." What's more, the study states that the "repetition of the same opinion gives rise to the impression that the opinion is widely shared, even if all the repetitions come from the same single communicator."[1] In short, the more people hear a message, the more it resonates with them. Does this mean that spokespeople should be like a "dog with a bone" and deliver the same message over and over again? Of course not. But it does mean that a carefully crafted message that is repeated through the media can dramatically influence public beliefs and attitudes. This chapter will present rules for crafting effective messages, define different types and forms of media messages, and examine a template for creating messages that shape public opinion.

Messaging Maxims

In its most basic form, a message is information passed from a source to a receiver. In the corporate or public relations world, messages are an intentional form of communication that presents calculated information to a defined audience. That audience is generally made up of various stakeholders such as investors, retailers, customers, and critics. These messages can be used to put issues into context, build brand awareness, manage image, influence opinion, or develop customer relationships. Although that may sound complicated, there are some basic rules that ensure messages address key subjects and make an impact on stakeholders.

- Use simple words.
- Keep sentences short.
- Create stand-alone sentences.
- Avoid qualifiers.
- Scratch your "but."

The last rule is not a typo and is not meant to be funny. Okay, maybe it is meant to be funny, but it's still very important. All of these rules are critical for crafting clear and persuasive messages.

Use Simple Words

Using jargon or buzzwords can make your messages appear convoluted, overly technical, or even patronizing. In responding to customer complaints about online booking problems, Virgin Trains stated, "Moving forward, we at Virgin Trains are looking to take ownership of the flow in question to apply our pricing structure, thus resulting in this journey search appearing in the new category—matrix format. The pricing of this particular flow is an issue going back to 1996 and it is not something that we can change until 2008 at the earliest. I hope this makes the situation clear."[2] To be honest, they lost me at "flow in question."

Compare that to Steven Jobs's response to early adopters upset by Apple reducing the price of the 8GB iPhone by two hundred dollars: "First, I am sure that we are making the correct decision to lower the price of the 8GB iPhone from $599 to $399, and that now is the right time to do it," wrote Jobs. "iPhone is a breakthrough product, and we have the chance to 'go for it' this holiday season. iPhone is so far ahead of the competition and now it will be affordable by even more customers. It benefits both Apple and every iPhone user to get as many customers as possible in the iPhone 'tent.' We strongly believe the $399 price will help us do just that this holiday season."[3] By using clear, straightforward language to share the rationale for lowering the iPhone price, Jobs was able to both mollify disgruntled customers and advance the discussion.

Marketing spokespeople use terms such as "value proposition" in their messaging, while those with technical backgrounds talk about how their products provide "solutions." These are two examples of "buzzwords" that are so overused that they lack meaning. BuzzWhack (www.buzzwhack.com) defines a buzzword as "a usually important sounding word or phrase used primarily to impress laypersons." Direct from BuzzWhack's website, here are some of the most dreadful buzzwords as voted on by the website's readers: leveraging our assets, mission-critical, information touch point, relanguage, and critical path.[4]

You can probably think of many more buzzwords or jargony terms that you've heard circulating in offices, meeting rooms, and professional conferences. Maybe you have even used some of these terms or phrases while communicating with colleagues or clients. However, the simple fact is that media messages are intended to connect with and appeal to a broad group of stakeholders. Using simple language will reduce the risk of confusion, increase the accessibility of your message, and make your words sound more sincere.

Keep Sentences Short

Newsmakers feel obliged to speak in long sentences for a variety of reasons, in part because they usually want to include as much relevant information as possible in each sentence since their peers will read their quotes and they don't want to appear glib; while, at the same time, other people rely on using long sentences because they don't know what they want to say, so they drone on in the hope they will stumble upon the point, and even if they do, chances are the reporter will find it extremely difficult to isolate a quote from their lengthy sentence.

Wow. With its one hundred words, the previous sentence winded me just writing it. Besides, if a reporter's question is answered in a sentence with a hundred words, it is unlikely the journalist will quote all one hundred words. Chances are ten of those words may be quoted, and in all likelihood, those ten words will not appropriately reflect the context of your message.

Instead of answering a journalist's question with a one-hundred-word sentence, deliver ten sentences of about ten words each. The key is to use short sentences and not give short answers, unless called for. Short answers can come across as terse and defensive, whereas short sentences are focused. Short sentences demonstrate clarity of thought. They have impact. They are quotable. The obvious exception to the short sentence rule is the Problem Solution Formula message described in the previous chapter.

To keep sentences short, make your point, put a period in there, and make your next point. Sometimes, this is easier said than done. During stressful situations, many people's minds begin racing. This means they form thoughts faster than their mouths can form words. People then try to recalibrate by using the word "and" to transition to the next thought. Only, many

Three Is the Magic Number

A two-point plan is not as quotable as a three-point plan, but four points are too many. A shopping list message with too many items buries concepts and ideas. Also, when providing a three-point plan, establish all your points before examining each in detail. For example: "Computerizing a patient's medical records will improve health care. First, an electronic health record system is good for patients. Second, electronic health records will save health care dollars. Third, lives will literally be saved by electronic health records. Now let me talk more about each point." Notice how easy it is to identify the main points. When you group your opening like this, it provides journalists with a ready-made quote and allows you to offer greater context as the answer unfolds.

times a next thought is nowhere to be found. To help limit sentence length, be mindful of conjunctions and conjunctive adverbs— words like *and, which, rather, however, because, nonetheless*—all of which make the ends of sentences elusive. Conjunctions and conjunctive adverbs weaken the focus of a media message and leave spokespeople vulnerable to saying something they later regret.

Create Stand-Alone Sentences

Simply put, a stand-alone sentence is a phrase, thought, sentence, or quote that can be understood independently of what came before it and what comes after it. Stand-alone sentences help newsmakers manage context. Stand-alone sentences ensure that each sentence makes sense on its own. Stand-alone sentences minimize opportunities for quotes to be taken out of context.

Often, people feel the need to respond to media questions in a linked or interreliant sequence. However, doing so can expose a message to the harsh realities of the editing process. By weaving sentences together and making one reliant on the other, a spokesperson's individual statements can end up making little sense on their own. Consider the following four sentences that comment on government policies to teach developmentally delayed children: "We disagree. If we do this the way they want us to, it won't work. Teaching developmentally delayed children must be done in a thoughtful way. Our approach is to work closer with parents and teachers to ensure the needs of developmentally delayed youngsters are met."

The problem is that sentence number one is incomplete until you hear sentence number two, which by itself makes no sense until you hear sentence number three. The final payoff to the response comes in sentence number four. If you attempt to build a case through interdependent sentences, you risk opening tomorrow's paper and seeing sentence number two ("If we do this the way they want us to, it won't work") as the only quote used, leading you to predictably exclaim, "Where's the rest of what I said? They took me out of context!"

Because spokespeople never know which sentences or quotes will permeate the media filter, their challenge is to ensure that every sentence makes complete sense on its own. Here is an example of an answer that contains stand-alone sentences:

Question: Does your company have a poor reputation when it comes to diversity?
Answer: At ACME Industries, we are proud of our commitment to diversity. When it comes to diversity, we hold ourselves to a high standard of integrity. Being a strong supporter of diversity is important to the way we do business.

Regardless of which sentence the reporter chooses to quote for the article, the question is answered in a coherent and thoughtful manner that presents ACME in a positive way. To ensure messages and answers have context, create each sentence as a stand-alone sentence.

Avoid Qualifiers

A qualifier is a word or phrase that limits the scope of an assertion or alters the meaning of other words in a sentence. Often, qualifiers are used to hedge or moderate a statement. Specifically, I am referring to phrases like "I think," "I believe," "I feel," and "I hope." When you use these types of phrases, it indicates that you're not certain of what you're stating. A comment like "I think we're a global leader in antivirus software" implies doubt. Whereas, a statement like "We are a global leader in antivirus software" conveys conviction. Leaving off qualifiers like "I think," "I feel," and "I believe" represents the difference between an opinion and a fact. To sound confident and assured, be mindful not to use qualifiers.

Scratch Your "But"

Spokespeople say "but" far too much, and often with harmful consequences. The word "but" has two negative impacts. First, it negates the goodwill that preceded it. Consider a statement like, "Our government supports initiatives to house the homeless, but. . . ." Can anything positive follow a setup like that? It's similar to a husband telling his wife, "I love your hair, but. . . ." The second problem with the word "but" is that it signals that an excuse is following. For example, "It's true we went over budget on the construction project, but it's due to the rising cost of materials." This statement sounds defensive. The solution in this case is to drop the word "but" and replace it with the word "and." "Yes, it's true we went over budget on the construction project and it's due to the rising cost of materials." With that one small change, the tone of the answer shifts from sounding like an excuse to sounding like an explanation.

The word "however" has the same negative effect as "but." For sentences that you believe need a word like "but" or "however," consider the following two options: start the sentence with the word "though." For example, "Though we ran over budget, it happened because we changed the scope of the project." The other alternative is to separate the message into two sentences: "The government supports initiatives to house the homeless. Our concern is whether the government's particular plan offers the best way to help the homeless meet their needs."

An exception to the Scratch Your But rule occurs when "but" helps you make your point. For instance, "The FDA has approved a lifesaving wonder drug, but the drug is too expensive for patients to obtain." Here, I've deliberately negated the goodwill that precedes the word "but" because the situation calls for it. Without the word "but," the focus of the message would be on the positive news of the drug approval, not its inaccessibility due to cost.

Does It Pass the "Says So-and-So" Test?

To determine if your messages are user-friendly, say them out loud and at the end of the message, add the words "says *so-and-so*." For instance, "Media messages must be compelling," says Ansell. Adding "says Ansell" helps you determine whether the message will read well in tomorrow's paper. The following sentence is an example of a message that does not roll off the tongue with ease: "People who require access to the judicial system should be provided with an appropriate level of resources to ensure they have opportunities for legal representation so they can be better served by the courts," says Ansell. Compare that mouthful to this version of the quote: "Everyone deserves legal counsel," says Ansell.

Media Message Types

Messages are what you want the media to report. They are, in essence, the quotes you want to see yourself delivering to reporters and stakeholders. By preparing messages before media interviews, spokespeople have the opportunity to influence the story the reporter writes. Creating these messages also makes reporters' jobs easier by giving them what they need to craft their stories. If spokespeople fail to prepare their messages in advance of media interviews, it leaves them vulnerable and only able to respond to questions without presenting their own agenda. In which case, the risk is that spokespeople may not have *their* story told.

There is no one-size-fits-all solution, however, for media messages. Different stories and situations call for specific types of messages that provide journalists with the quotes they need to report the news. Message types include those that tell your story, offer facts, provide perspective, show concern, and move people to act. In some cases the different message types are best used together, while at other times there is a need to select the message types most suitable for a specific situation. The following sections examine the most effective types of media messages, explain their usage, and offer real-world examples of each.

"Your News Is" Message

The Your News Is message must be from your perspective, not that of others. If a special-interest group wrongly accuses your company of poisoning the river, the news may be "ACME Industries accused of poisoning the local river." But that's not your news. Your news is "We are proud of our environmental initiatives." That's providing this is true, of course. Some more examples include these:

The news: ACME agrees to pay smaller firm $500 million in patent settlement.
Your news: This settlement paves the way for the two companies to collaborate and innovate.
The news: Warm weather leaves no snow for Olympic downhill event.

Your news: Even with the mild weather, we have all the technology, people, and expertise to deliver a first-class event.
The news: Oil company to slash refining jobs.
Your news: Streamlining the refining division will let us compete better in the future.

In crafting a Your News Is message, imagine it will be the only message the media will report. Therefore, it must be able to convey the essence of your story, ideally in one simply worded and short sentence. The "Your News Is" message must get to the heart of your story and provide people with the information, perspective, or emotion you want them to encounter once they see or hear it.

Tell Your Story Message

Frequently, news reports feature three quotes from the principal newsmaker. If that's you, it's important to be both proactive and succinct. Reporters have little desire to wade through a mass of information in the hope of picking out a few sentences that represent the salient points of your story. To help exert greater influence over how your story is told, be able to tell it in three simply worded and short sentences. Using the tobacco industry as an example, here are three short sentences about the sector's place in the American economy:

- "Tobacco is a legal product."
- "Tobacco is used by 20 percent of the adult population."
- "Well over two-thirds of the cost of a package of cigarettes is taxes."

Regardless of which quote the journalist selects, the spokesperson's point is made. The Tell Your Story Message is of particular value for brief interviews in which reporters are simply looking for a couple of quotes for their story.

What News Means to Stakeholders Message

In identifying which stories to report, journalists, editors, and producers need to have a sense of who is affected by the news in question. To qualify as news, the story must matter to someone, somewhere. This message identifies the impact your news or story has on other people. Does your news offer information that is meaningful, interesting, or useful? Does your story directly affect people's lives? Here are three examples of the What News Means to Stakeholders message:

Story: Federal regulators offer incentives for cooperation in probes.
What news means to stakeholders: People can now avoid jail and civil claims by helping regulators investigating cases.
Story: Company rejects hostile takeover attempt.
What news means to stakeholders: Shareholders deserve more money for their shares.
Story: Wireless companies call for usage pricing.
What news means to stakeholders: We'll need to bill folks the same way as water and power companies.

Fact Message

Without facts, news is about guesses, hunches, and gossip. Reporters need facts to frame and write their stories. Mostly, fact messages are numbers, statistics, dates, and percentages. Facts work especially well when newsmakers need to demonstrate mastery over information. For example, if a health care critic claims that people without proper insurance are being turned away from hospital emergency rooms, facts and statistics are needed to prove it.

Facts are also useful in persuading people to look at particular issues in a different light. Recognizing that the public feels it is being fleeced on gasoline prices, a leading oil company in Canada launched a campaign to offer perspective on pricing.

Petro-Canada reported that around 45 percent of the cost of a liter of gas is used to capture the crude oil; 32 percent of the cost goes to taxes; and 20 percent is spent refining, transporting, distributing, marketing, and retailing the gas. Petro-Canada used facts to prove to consumers that its retail profit in 2007 was about 3 percent of the average pump price.[5] Upon hearing those statistics, consumers may not have gained greater sympathy for the oil companies, but at least they knew the facts on pricing. Here are a few examples of fact messages using quarterly numbers provided by the Newspaper Association of America as a theme:

- "Newspapers across the country earned $623 million in online advertising."[6]
- "Newspaper websites attracted 74 million visitors."
- "Visitors to newspaper websites spent 2.7 billion minutes browsing the sites."[7]

Facts provide an accurate, unbiased representation of an issue or situation, but facts by themselves do not tell a complete story. At best, facts are one- or two-dimensional and leave much open to interpretation. That is why journalists often look to experts and analysts to provide interpretation of facts—thus the need for what I call color messages.

Color Message

Sporting events on television are usually hosted by two types of announcers. The first type offers a play-by-play description of everything that happens on the field. This announcer provides the "facts" of the game. The second type of announcer provides what is commonly called "color commentary." This includes offering an interpretation of the game, the individual plays, and the performance of its players. Similarly, the color message is designed to enhance the fact message. This type of message provides interpretation of a story's facts and expresses concern for those affected by it. In addition, color messages provide an opportunity to relate facts to values and offer an illustrative means for understanding complex or unfamiliar concepts. There are four different types of color messages: Context Color message, Concern Color message, Absolute Color message, and Figurative Color message. Here is a brief summary of the four types:

- **Context Color message** interprets and explains what facts mean.
- **Concern Color message** tells people you care.
- **Absolute Color message** responds to relentless attack or highlights values.
- **Figurative Color message** creates a word picture and simplifies a complex message.

Some news stories call for messages from all four categories. Other news stories require just one or two of the message types. To determine which types of color messages are called for in a given situation, here is an explanation of each category and suggestions for when to use them.

Context Color Message.   Just as the name implies, a Context Color message adds context to a Fact Message. It embraces theme, meaning, and interpretation to explain what the facts mean. The Context Color message is particularly valuable for stories containing complex facts. For example: "The packaging of the genomic DNA into chromatin in the cell nucleus requires machinery that facilitates DNA-dependent processes such as transcription in the presence of repressive chromatin structures." In this instance, the following would be an appropriate Context Color message: "Dividing human cells is a tricky process."

How's the Weather?

An easy way to remember how to create Context Color messages is to use the weather as an illustration. Consider these weather facts:

- Today, it is 75 degrees.
- Winds are southwest at 45 miles an hour.
- The chance of rain is 25 percent.

Context Color messages that capture the context of these weather facts are

- It's a nice day today.
- It's windy out.
- It might rain.

When writing a weather story, the journalist would likely quote the Context Color message and paraphrase the facts to read, "According to Ansell, there is a 25 percent chance of rain. 'It might rain today,' said Ansell."

Here are a few more examples of fact messages and corresponding Context Color messages:

Fact: Three million dollars has been spent on this safety initiative.
Context: This new safety program is a good investment.
Fact: Recycling programs diverted twenty-five tons of waste from dump sites.
Context: Environmental programs are important to the community.
Fact: Our power transmission reliability rate is 99 percent.
Context: We provide homeowners with safe, reliable power.

Though fact and Context Color messages generally work well in separate sentences, there are circumstances in which they work better together. For example, if reporters question your intention to purchase a company that is underperforming in the marketplace, your response requires context:

Question: How much are you planning to offer to purchase the company?
Answer: $40 million.

The answer reflects the "fact" portion of the response, but the answer by itself will lead to further questions about the wisdom of the purchase. What's missing in the answer is context.

Question: How much are you planning to offer to purchase the company?
Answer: For the $40 million we're willing to pay, we will have access to a new product line and manufacturing facilities that will return far more value than our initial investment.

Rather than just serving up numbers and statistics, use Context Color messages to wrap context and perspective around your facts.

Concern Color Message.   Sometimes people just want someone to listen to them and understand their angst. Recently, my smartphone mysteriously erased my task list, which helps organize my daily activities. I was extremely upset. I contacted a call center representative responsible for handling such concerns. During the call I let my feelings get the best of me and spoke in a manner that resulted in the call center representative telling me not to raise my voice. That's when I became really angry. I felt that the person on the other end had no idea of the impact of losing all the items in my to-do list. It made me feel as if he was not the one to help solve my problem. In fact, no one was able to fix my problem. However, some recognition of my angst from the call center representative would have helped me feel better.

The Concern Color message shows that you empathize with others, especially when they are negatively affected by something you may have done or that may have occurred under your supervision. If, for instance, the flu has claimed the lives of several residents of the nursing home you operate, an example of a Concern Color message would be, "We're deeply saddened by this loss of life."

Concern Color messages exist on a sliding scale. For instance, if employees or customers are killed, spokespeople must express their deep "sadness" for such a "tragic" and "devastating" event. In this type of terrible situation, the Concern Color message is a vital component of any response. But if someone slips on a wet floor and breaks a leg, words or phrases like "unfortunate," "lamentable," and "sincerely regret" are more appropriate. Accordingly, if employees go on strike, spokespeople can be "upset" that customers are "inconvenienced" and "worried" about labor-management relations.

In tragic situations where there is an employee death, the Concern Color message must convey warmth. For instance, if two employees have died in a workplace accident, consider these choices: "ACME Industries is devastated by what happened to our colleagues." Or, "We're devastated by what happened to our colleagues." In this case, using "we" instead of "ACME Industries" has a warmer, more genuine sound to it. Using first-person plural pronouns like "we," "us," and "our" instead of a company's name makes messages sound more inclusive and heartfelt.

In situations involving unproven allegations, it is still appropriate to be disturbed. For example, an allegation of sexual harassment in your office should have you "concerned" or "troubled." The Concern Color message is of use even in situations where you may feel concern is not warranted. For instance, if a fringe environmental group believes vapors from your plant harm the community's worm population, the group's concerns must still be treated with respect. Even though you may feel the concern expressed is trivial and ridiculous, it is nevertheless worthy of acknowledgment. To say "We understand this is a concern for some folks" does not mean you lend credence to a specious or absurd claim. If anything, it shows you have respect for the beliefs of others.

Absolute Color Message. The Absolute Color message provides spokespeople with an opportunity to identify shared concerns with other parties and assert their values at the same time. The Absolute Color message is intended to ratchet down controversy. Many large companies, organizations, and governments tend to make bad news worse by arguing with critics. Rather than make a bad situation worse, the Absolute Color message serves to build common ground, providing spokespeople with an opportunity to identify shared values with other parties. It demonstrates to critics and stakeholders that you appreciate the significance of what has taken place, especially when your company or organization is under attack.

Imagine your company has just had a major chemical spill. Hazardous compounds including nickel and cadmium have spilled into the local river. Greenpeace is protesting outside your plant, calling your company an "environmental criminal." An example of an Absolute Color message to use in this situation is, "The environment must be protected." Did you expect me to say the environment must be protected? My guess is you did not. Was I wrong to say the environment must be protected? No. Who, if anybody, would you expect to say, "The environment must be protected"? If you answered Greenpeace, you're right. In fact, after hearing the comment, Greenpeace officials would likely say, "Hey, that's our line." But it is true, the environment must be protected. No one can argue against it. It is an absolute.

There are no two ways about an Absolute Color message. You cannot argue against it because it is an absolute, much like the following:

- Inner-city housing prices must be affordable.
- Medicines must be safe.
- Employees must be treated well.

Compare the following two quotes: "The environment must be protected," and "We must protect the environment." Does the second quote qualify as an Absolute Color message? It could, but the question of who is "we" remains ambiguous. Is "we" the company or is it "we" the people? True Absolute Color messages should not, as a rule, make use of pronouns like "I," "us," "we," or "our," or the name of the company you represent. To be considered a true Absolute Color message, it should read, "The environment must be protected."

Absolute Color Message Words

Absolute Color messages need punch. An Absolute Color message that reads "Sustainable development is a priority" is not nearly as powerful as "Sustainable development must be a priority." Forceful words to help create Absolute Color messages include the following:

- *Must:* "Companies must be ethical."
- *Need:* "Communities need a clean environment."
- *Deserve:* "Everyone deserves fair treatment."
- *Expect:* "Employees expect fair wages."

There are two useful tricks you can use to help identify whether the message you create is an absolute or not. First, see if it sounds absurd when "not" is inserted into the message. For instance, it would sound ridiculous to say:

- Inner-city housing prices must *not* be affordable.
- Medicines must *not* be safe.
- Employees must *not* be treated well.

The second way to identify an Absolute Color message is to ask yourself whether you can visualize your critics delivering the same words in exactly the same way. I can certainly see critics making statements like "The environment must be protected" and "Medicines must be safe."

When an organization is attacked for an actual wrong it committed, the Absolute Color message stands as is. That is, if a government agency is proven to be wasting taxpayer money, the response begins with a Problem Solution Formula message (to admit and fix) and is then followed by an Absolute Color message: "Taxpayer dollars were not spent appropriately, and we will cooperate fully with government auditors to ensure there is integrity to the process. Taxpayer dollars must be well spent." On the other hand, if an allegation that government tax dollars are poorly spent is unfounded, then the Absolute Color message is revised to read, "Taxpayer dollars must be well spent, and they are." Adding the extra words of affirmation at the end of the Absolute Color message ensures the point of propriety is made.

Absolute Color messages need not be more than four to seven words long. Spokespeople who have difficulty crafting Absolute Color messages can use the Context Color message as a gateway. For example, in a scenario that has shareholders complaining about a corporate acquisition not in the best interests of the company, an appropriate Context Color message would be "We make acquisitions that offer value for the long term." Then, turn that Context Color message into "Acquisitions must offer value." Now you have an effective Absolute Color message that cannot be denied or disputed.

Figurative Color Message.   This type of message uses phrases or figures of speech that achieve their effect through association, comparison, and resemblance. They're often vivid, convenient ways of explaining complex ideas or encapsulating multifaceted issues. They do so by providing an instant word picture, like the one from Russia's Vladimir Putin. Responding to press allegations about his personal fortune, Putin said the report was "muck picked out of someone's nose and smeared on paper."[8] Not a pretty picture, but a picture nonetheless. Figurative Color messages comprise four basic figures of speech:

- Idioms
- Metaphors
- Similes
- Analogies

An idiom is a descriptive phrase that has a different meaning than its individual parts would indicate. It can create this meaning through a picture or exaggerated image that describes a specific action or event. Some examples of idioms include these:

- Burn the candle at both ends.
- Grab the bull by the horns.
- Fall asleep at the switch.

In the preceding examples, the images figuratively equate to working too hard, taking charge of a problem, and being inattentive. Due to their utility and convenience, many idioms have become clichés.

A metaphor is an implicit comparison made between two unlike things that actually have something in common. In simple terms, a metaphor states, "X is Y." Examples of metaphors include these:

- Business success is a constant battle.
- Karen in Accounting is a machine.
- ACME Industries is a big fish in a small pond.

These metaphors vividly depict the difficult nature of business success, Karen's machinelike efficiency, and ACME's dominance in a limited market. Because metaphors assert two things are the same (X is Y), they are the most direct type of Figurative Color message.

A simile is a type of metaphor, but it makes its comparison more explicit by using words "like" or "as." In simple terms, a simile states "X is *like* Y." Here are three examples of similes:

- In some parts of the world, guns are like cell phones.
- Tom was as quiet as a mouse.
- Sarah was like a shark smelling blood in the water.

The benefit of this construction is that it allows the two ideas or objects being compared to remain distinct. Guns aren't actually like cell phones. You can't call someone with a gun. It's just that in some parts of the world, guns are ubiquitous. Accordingly, similes are best used to imply a limited similarity or reflect a simple or singular comparison.

Like metaphors and similes, analogies compare dissimilar objects or events. However, while metaphors and similes are usually descriptive, analogies are used to make a logical connection, argue a position, or make something complex more understandable. In essence, an analogy infers that if two things are alike in some ways, they must also be alike in other ways. Analogies can be short, but in many cases they take the form of extended metaphors or similes. U.S. Representative James Greenwood delivered a triple-header analogy when he told Enron accountant David Duncan, "Mr. Duncan, Enron robbed the bank, Arthur Anderson provided the getaway car, and they say you were at the wheel."[9] In a MediaStrategies training program for an antivirus software company in Silicon Valley, an engineer (there is hope yet!) created a perfect analogy: "Our product is like a fortress, while everyone else's is like a picket fence." That single quote was reported worldwide.

Reporters eat up Figurative Color messages like candy. At a news conference I attended as a reporter, the spokesperson was failing to deliver a clear, concise message. We were there to write a story about a new product, but the messages she delivered were dull and uninspired. Suddenly, the spokesperson declared the new product would sell "faster than a chicken with the Colonel running after it" and the room came to life. We all scribbled in our pads "chicken—Colonel—running" and featured the quote in our stories.

Figurative Color messages are best used in good news stories and must be avoided like the plague in bad news stories. What are you going to say in a bad news story, "They're dropping like flies"? It won't work. Bad news Figurative Color messages to stay away from include the following:

- It's a sinking ship.
- It's a train wreck.
- They're running around like chickens with their heads cut off.

There is an exception to the rule, however. When I trained a group of nuclear plant operators to talk about a radiation leak, one of their messages stated, "One REM per hour of radiation was released." How much is one REM of radiation? Is it harmful? Is it deadly? In this case, an appropriate Figurative Color message would be, "Exposure to one REM per hour of radiation is like getting a chest X-ray." Now I feel safer.

Call to Action Message

"Just say no to mosquito spraying" is a message that calls people to action. A Call to Action message is just that—a rallying cry for people to act on information they have just heard. It is designed to get people to do something as a result of what you have told them. People who read or watch the news sometimes feel strongly about a story they see or hear, so much so that they want to become a part of the story and help in some way. The Call to Action Message tells them how they can become involved. Special-interest groups are especially effective in issuing calls to action, particularly on matters where the public is polarized. Consider the abortion debate. Pro-life and pro-choice advocates each know how to tap into the sentiments of their stakeholders and get them to act, whether it's through a protest or an online petition.

A Call to Action message is particularly useful in situations where pressure needs to be applied, especially on government or a sector of industry. For instance, when forty mayors from around the globe gathered to meet about global warming, they urged G8 leaders "to commit to a long-term goal for the stabilization of atmospheric greenhouse gas concentrations." As former London mayor and group spokesman Ken Livingstone said, "This is a clear wake-up call for the G8."[10]

If Asked Message

When crafting messages for the media, spokespeople focus mostly on the information and the quotes they want reported. Their objective is to use their messages to tell their story. But journalists have a responsibility to probe newsmakers and ask questions that make spokespeople feel uncomfortable. In those situations, the solution is not to use messages that bear little resemblance to the issue or question causing the discomfort. Instead, the solution is to be ready by having a message prepared for the difficult or discomforting question. The If Asked message is the message spokespeople use to address questions or matters they don't want to bring up but know the reporter will. For example, if a political candidate discussing his platform suspects he will be asked about drug use as a youth, he will use the If Asked message to address it. When that very subject came up at a meeting with magazine editors, then-senator Barack Obama was ready with a response: "When I was a kid, I inhaled," he said. "It was reflective of the struggles and confusion of a teenage boy. Teenage boys are frequently confused."[11]

The Compelling Message Creator

Knowing what you want to say is essential when engaging journalists. The Compelling Message Creator is a one-page template that provides a process for crafting quotable messages that meet the needs of journalists and assure you the opportunity to present your agenda in a proactive manner. By bringing together various message types and ingredients, it can be used to prepare messages for both good news and bad news situations. A reproducible copy of the Compelling Message Creator can be found in the Appendix.

Since its initial creation, the Compelling Message Creator has constantly evolved to better reflect the elements reporters require when crafting their stories. Currently, many professional spokespeople successfully use the template on a daily basis and in media reports worldwide.

To complete the Compelling Message Creator, start by transferring your Value Compass words from Chapter Two. Then, if you are facing a bad-news situation or widespread criticism, transfer your Problem Solution Formula message from Chapter Three. After that, fill in the blanks provided for each type of message. For definitions and examples of each type of message, refer to the preceding section, "Media Message Types." The explanations and examples in that section correspond directly to the template format. To see an example of a completed Compelling Message Creator, continue to the next section.

Biojax Part 4: The Compelling Message Creator in Practice

In the opening chapter, we met Joan Smith, chief executive officer of JLA Life Sciences Corporation, maker of the very expensive cancer drug Biojax. When we first met her, Joan was being interviewed about the price and availability of Biojax. The news story that resulted from her interview highlighted a number of negative quotes that tarnished her company's image in the media. As a reminder, here are some of the quotes that were reported:

- "It's not as if Biojax is dangerous or unproven."
- "We are not greedy."
- "We are not letting people die."

In a Chapter Six interview do-over, Joan will be asked the same tough questions. What will change, however, are her responses. Knowing what attributes she wants to project in her responses, Joan used the directions and examples provided in the previous "Media Message Types" section to prepare the Compelling Message Creator shown in the following sidebar.

Joan's Compelling Message Creator for Biojax

The News Is . . . JLA Life Sciences Corporation is accused of greed in pricing its new biologic cancer drug.

Value Compass Words (Chapter Two)

Empathetic	Anger	Education	Ethical
N	E	W	S

Problem Solution Formula Message (Chapter Three): Unfortunately, Biojax is expensive due to the high cost of manufacturing medicine made from living cells, so government needs to help patients battling cancer by offering coverage for this important medicine.

Your News Is . . . Patients are being denied access to Biojax, a new drug that slows the growth of cancer for some patients, helping them live longer.

Tell Your Story in Three Short Sentences:
1. Biojax is a highly effective cancer fighting drug.
2. People with cancer could live longer by taking Biojax, but government won't help.
3. We wish this cancer medicine could be less expensive.

What the News Means to Stakeholders Message: Cancer patients are suffering because of a bureaucratic decision not to reimburse them for a new drug that could possibly help them.

Three Fact Messages:
1. Eighteen hundred patients were involved in clinical studies for Biojax.
2. The growth of cancer slowed for 60 percent of the patients using Biojax.
3. Forty percent of patients rely on government to pay for the medicines they use.

Context Color Message: Government should support cancer patients who can be helped by Biojax.

Concern Color Message: Our hope is to see this medicine in the hands of those who need it.

Absolute Color Message: Cancer patients must have access to medicines that work.

Figurative Color Message: Cancer patients without a private drug plan are like passengers on the *Titanic*—the lifeboats are only available to passengers who can afford them.

Call to Action Message: Patients should call or write their representatives to push them to help pay for this important, new drug.

"If Asked . . ." Message:
If asked: Will you abandon patients who need Biojax, but can't afford it?
Answer: Through our Compassionate Care Program, we do our very best to help as many patients as we can.

Armed with a comprehensive selection of compelling messages, Joan now needs to learn how to effectively deliver these messages. In the next chapter, I'll explain how to manage nervousness, use body language and vocal inflection, and avoid common presentation mistakes in order to optimize message delivery.

Chapter Talking Points

- Using simple words and simple language in your messages will reduce the risk of confusion, increase the accessibility of your message, and make your words sound more sincere.

- Keep your sentences short. Instead of answering a journalist's question with a one-hundred-word sentence, deliver ten sentences of about ten words each.

- Create stand-alone sentences in order to ensure messages and answers have context.

- Leaving off qualifiers like "I think," "I feel," and "I believe" represents the difference between an opinion and a fact. To sound confident and assured, be mindful not to use qualifiers.

- Spokespeople say "but" far too much, and often with harmful consequences. The word "but" has two negative impacts: it negates the goodwill that precedes it and it signals that an excuse is following.

- The Compelling Message Creator, found in the Appendix, is a one-page template that provides a process for crafting quotable messages that meet the needs of journalists and assure you the opportunity to present your agenda in a proactive and positive manner.

5

DELIVERING YOUR MESSAGE

"I'm going to be a lot more careful about
everything I say, because I find that it gets
amplified to a new level."
          —*Mike Huckabee, former presidential candidate*

Words are like toothpaste. Once you squeeze them out, you can't get them back into the tube. As George Smitherman, Ontario's former deputy premier, lamented, "At the heart of it, you say a million words and some of them you wish that you could take back."[1] When answering questions from the media, a spokesperson must control every word. This means both knowing what to say *and* how to say it. But the ability to think on your feet when reporters fire questions at you requires a composure and calmness that does not come naturally. Being forced to respond to challenging questions, sometimes under hot lights, is most unnerving. But unlike hitting a Major League fastball or becoming a concert pianist, effective message delivery is a skill that can be learned by anyone. Comprising primarily physical behaviors, the ability to speak with confidence and clarity can be developed through study and practice. The strategies and techniques presented in this chapter will help you use your voice, gestures, and natural energy to take control of your environment and optimize opportunities for message delivery. The chapter will also help you develop the skills you need to appear responsive and sincere, whether presenting a prepared statement, making impromptu remarks, or managing a contentious news conference.

Slow Your Racing Brain

The spokespeople I train tell me they want help learning how to think quickly on their feet. Sounds like a worthy objective, right? Wrong. People already think too quickly on their feet—that's the problem. Thinking quickly in stressful moments kicks people's brains into high gear. Hurriedly, they ask themselves, "What am I going to say next?" Spokespeople distracted by thinking about what's coming next lose control over what they say now. In truth, spokespeople need to think slowly on their feet. They need to decelerate their brains and gain mastery over every word. To do this, spokespeople need to learn to breathe properly and speak slowly.

Breathe In . . . Breathe Out

In anxious moments, our autonomic (involuntary) nervous system causes the release of stress-inducing hormones such as adrenaline, norepinephrine, and cortisol. These hormones trigger reflexive reactions, including an increased heart rate, raised blood pressure, pupil dilation, decreased saliva production, profuse sweating, and oxygen deprivation. In turn, these lead to an overwhelming acceleration in brain activity that often results in disorientation and the separation of cognitive functioning and verbal skills. Or in other words, a separation of the brain and tongue. Learning to breathe properly helps calm the autonomic nervous system and synchronize the brain and tongue to work in perfect unison.

Every human on the planet is born breathing in the same way, but by age three stress reverses normal breathing patterns. Consequently, most adults do not breathe properly. Ujai breathing, as taught in yoga, re-creates our original breathing patterns. Balancing and calming, it is a diaphragmatic breathing technique that first fills the lower belly, then rises through the chest. By increasing oxygenation and building internal body heat, it naturally relaxes the sympathetic, or panic-inducing, portion of the autonomic nervous system. To stay calm and focused during stressful situations, follow the Ujai breathing method:

> *Breathe in:* Belly out.
> *Breathe out:* Belly in.

Nice and slow.

> *Breathe in:* Belly out.
> *Breathe out:* Belly in.

Make every breath last three to five seconds.

> *Breathe in:* Belly out.
> *Breathe out:* Belly in.

See your stomach rise and fall with each slow breath you take.

> *Breathe in:* Belly out.
> *Breathe out:* Belly in.

Use your nose—it warms and filters the air.

> *Breathe in:* Belly out.
> *Breathe out:* Belly in.

If you can, try to breathe this way all the time. Practice helps considerably. Consider taking a yoga class or, at the very least, watching clips of correct Ujai breathing on the Internet. As you'll discover, proper breathing truly is the key to synchronizing mind and body. Within the context of a media interview, spokespeople must make sure they breathe correctly when listening to questions. The tough questions are the ones that make people stop breathing and default to a panicked, "What am I going to say?"

Speak Slowly

Hearing a spokesperson unleash a torrent of words is not by itself a giveaway that the individual is nervous. Often, people speak quickly to imply a sense of urgency or to reflect passion for the subject matter. But when spokespeople talk quickly to reporters, they risk experiencing brain-tongue separation, a verbal glitch where the brain and tongue disengage, resulting in words that leave your lips faster than you intended. Talking slowly helps you control what you say, as you say it.

Everyday conversation has the average person speaking at 175 words per minute. While pursuing the Democratic nomination, speeches by Barack Obama averaged 110 words per minute. Speaking in this type of thoughtful, deliberate manner adds "gravitas to the message almost regardless of what the message is," said speechwriter Dan McGroarty, who wrote for former president George H. W. Bush. In contrast, Hillary Clinton clocked in at an average of 188 words a minute in her campaign speeches. McGroarty told the *Globe and Mail* that "to be above 125, 130 is breakneck."[2]

Speaking slowly in stressful situations is easier said than done, however. To slow yourself down, slightly stretch the vowel sound in each word. Don't stretch the vowel to the point where it sounds ridiculous, but even a slight elongation will force you to linger over each word and produce a slower pace. Another way to slow yourself down is to make a concerted effort to pause between sentences, thoughts, and phrases.

Power of the Pause

Well-timed pauses are essential in delivering messages and presentations that engage people. While a speaker's words can drive away an audience, silence can recapture their attention. Sound counterintuitive? Imagine you're at a conference listening to a presenter who is trying to pack as much information as possible into his sixty-minute time slot. After a few minutes of listening to the presenter drone on and on, you're likely to start reading a newspaper or checking your e-mail. As one sentence runs into the next, pretty soon everyone in the audience is reading, looking at their smartphone, or thinking about what's for lunch. But what happens if the speaker suddenly stops talking? Everyone immediately looks up. The sudden silence captures everyone's attention because something important must be about to happen. Where an uninterrupted flow of words can disengage, the silence created by a well-timed pause engages.

Pausing also helps your messages penetrate by allowing audience members or reporters time to process your words and information. Therefore, after delivering an important point, pause for a second or two to let your words sink in and to highlight the significance of what you've said. Another benefit of pausing is that it acts as a quality-control measure, making you sound more articulate and convincing. Speaking quickly causes many spokespeople to use words or phrases like "uh," "um," or "you know" as a way of linking thoughts. Uttering these phrases makes a speaker appear inarticulate and is a clear indication that the brain has disconnected from the tongue. Better to pause, take a deep breath, and only say a word when you know precisely what you want to say. If you ever feel overwhelmed while being interviewed or speaking in front of an audience, recalibrate by breathing and pausing.

Body Language Speaks

There is more involved in delivering a message than simply saying it. Dr. Albert Mehrabian of the University of California at Los Angeles studied the impact body language has on the way people receive messages. In his research, Dr. Mehrabian has identified that when people speak, their message is interpreted not only through the words they use but also through the way they move their body, use their face, and inflect with their voice. According to his study, 55 percent of the way our message is interpreted comes through our body and face, while 38 percent comes through the inflection in our voices. Run the numbers and you'll see that leaves a whopping 7 percent of interpretation coming through the words we choose.[3] This means that nonverbal congruency and synchronicity are vital to the efficacy of communication, especially as it relates to media.

Body Language Determines an Election

In the 1992 campaign, President George H. W. Bush clearly looked at his watch during a live debate on national TV, and voters got the feeling he didn't want to be there. In that same debate, Bill Clinton walked over to a woman who had asked a question about the economy and looked her in the eye as he answered. In response, the woman nodded her head, affirming what she was hearing from the Democratic candidate. By narrowing the physical distance and using engaging body language, Clinton was able to give the impression of sharing both the issue and the solution with the questioner. According to pollster Frank Luntz, "That one small move led hundreds of thousands of people to change their minds" and vote for Clinton.[4]

Looking and sounding like you mean what you say involves the coordination of a number of body parts. Luckily, we as humans are constantly sending and receiving nonverbal signals during nearly all of our personal interactions. These signals include postures, gestures, facial expressions, and eye movements that ease mental effort when communication is difficult and facilitate comprehension while communicating complex feelings or concepts. For a message to be well-delivered and received, it must be communicated in a manner that brings together the visual, the vocal, and the verbal. In other words, you must coordinate how you look, how you sound, and what you say. There are a number of keys to controlling your face, body, and tone in order to successfully deliver the messages you have carefully crafted.

Use Your Face

Facial expression is one of the most prevalent and powerful channels of nonverbal communication. It can be used to modify speech, control conversation, convey personality, and express emotion. Consequently, spokespeople must look as if they're saying what they mean and mean what they're saying. Otherwise a mixed message is delivered, undermining the credibility of both the messenger and the message. For instance, if your face naturally defaults to a smile there will be a disconnect if, during a media interview, you smile while discussing a serious issue or subject.

To achieve congruency when juggling the visual component, always let the look on your face match the mood and tone of what you are saying, as you are saying it. If your message is happy or positive, smile as you talk. If you, like me, are unable to smile on cue, then simply lift your eyebrows as you speak, which in turn will lift your face. This gives the impression of a relaxed, upbeat demeanor. If your message is sad or negative, however, furrow your brow as you speak to demonstrate your concern. If your message is designed to sound tough, tilt your head down slightly and roll your eyes up, as if you're latching onto someone with your gaze. For additional information on facial expressions and how they relate to emotions, I encourage you to refer to the works of Dr. Paul Ekman. Besides publishing a number of groundbreaking books and articles on the subject, he also maintains an interactive website that explores both the utility and interpretation of facial expressions.

The Eyes Have It

Our eyes are one of our greatest communication tools. They reveal thoughts and feelings and help us better understand one another. They also help create a bond between speaker and audience. Whether you realize it or not, every form of oratory communication is actually a two-way dialogue—even speeches, lectures, and presentations. One person sends a message and another person receives it. Eye contact guarantees this two-way communication has taken place. By looking at your audience, you can see whether listeners are engaged or not. Are they interested in what you're saying? Do they understand your messages?

To ensure you're engaging an audience, deliver one complete thought to one face or one part of the room before shifting eye contact. An audience essentially breaks down into three parts: the people in front of you, the people to your right, and the people to your left. Try to make eye contact in all three areas of the audience so everyone feels included. This technique is effective whether you're speaking to three reporters or a crowd of three hundred protestors. During a news conference or a question-and-answer period, make eye contact with the person asking you a question, then maintain eye contact as you answer. If, however, you broaden your answer and direct it to others in the audience, begin by looking at the questioner, then shift your eye contact throughout the entire group to engage the audience as a whole.

Talk with Your Hands

Contrary to what others may have told you, it is appropriate to use your hands when you talk. Hands are a wonderful visual aid. They help animate you as you speak, adding life and movement to your words. Too many interviewees muzzle their hands when they speak, likely because they were told to do so either by a parent, teacher, or communications consultant. But in truth, using your hands as you talk makes you look natural. People speak using their hands in everyday conversation, so why should a media interview be any different? When a spokesperson keeps her hands firmly in place, all the anxiety that goes along with talking to the media has no way of escaping her body. Anxiety that does not get released ricochets from head to toe and back again, causing further anxiety. Using your hands when you talk helps release the anxiety, almost as if you were shaking it away.

Hand movements also help those who tend to speak in a monotone have greater vocal inflection, which helps spokespeople deliver messages that sound distinct. Like a conductor controlling an orchestra, you can use your hands to help control your pace, inflection, and tone. To do so, make your hands match the rhythm of your words. Start with your fingers open, slightly spread, and slightly curled, then move your hands in a firm, deliberate motion. As you speak, change the motion to match your content. If you're exploring an idea or concept in greater depth, use a rolling gesture. If you're comparing two distinct concepts or examples, shift your hands from one side of your body to the other. If you're making an apology or expressing contrition, hold your hands out with your palms up. Using these types of deliberate, expressive hand gestures will actually force you to put more energy and passion into your words so that the vocal matches the visual. You see, the hand bone is connected to the voice bone.

Beware of Body Language Leakage

When people become anxious, their bodies tighten and they begin to engage in involuntary or unconscious movements. Some people play with their hair, others their glasses. Even former President Bill Clinton, who has masterful body language, was seen repeatedly scratching his nose while appearing before

Kenneth Starr's investigative committee. When people lie, their capillaries expand, making the nose itchy. The body doesn't lie.

One of the most prominent forms of leakage is the head nod. Within the context of media interviews, a nodding head gives the impression you agree with what is being said, even though you may not. For instance, imagine your head is bobbing up a storm while the reporter asks, "The concern on Wall Street is that as CEO, you have run this business into the ground and have caused irreparable harm to shareholders. What is your comment?" If you nod while listening to this question, the journalist could write, "Ansell nodded yes when presented with evidence of his failure."

There are at least two reasons why people nod when listening to others. First, the head nod is often delivered as a sign that "I'm listening" or "I care." But sometimes, people nod their heads when listening as a nonverbal way of telling the other person to hurry up and finish talking, so they can jump back in to control the conversation. Regardless, try to avoid nodding your head while listening to a question from a reporter.

Another common form of leakage is the "swallow," which affects everyone, but is mostly noticeable in men. The swallow usually occurs after a hard-hitting question is asked and the respondent swallows in an exaggerated fashion, as if he's been caught in a bluff. When men swallow this way, it's almost as if their Adam's apple is bobbing up and down, announcing to the world, "You got me." Gulping in this manner is an involuntary action, and as such it's difficult to control. But that doesn't mean you need to let other people see it. When you have the urge to nervously swallow, dip your head down to conceal the swallow, then quickly lift your head back up when you're done.

By the way, sometimes you may feel the need to swallow because of a buildup of saliva in your mouth. As an alternative to swallowing, try placing the tip of your tongue behind your two front teeth and then breathe in through your mouth. The saliva quickly disappears and the mouth dries up. What do you do when your mouth gets too dry and you need saliva? Gently bite the inside of your cheek. This creates saliva.

Likewise, be mindful not to purse your lips after completing an answer. When spokespeople are uncomfortable, they tend to press their lips together at the end of their answer, as if to signal to the questioner, "That's all I'm going to say; now you talk." Better to leave your lips slightly ajar. To control this and other forms of inappropriate body language, simply remember to breathe properly and use your hands to talk so you can expel your leakage before it expels itself in a way you cannot control.

Vocal Motion

How you use your voice is critical to how your message is received. Getting the tone right is important in establishing and supporting your intended meaning. A loud, clear voice indicates strength and conviction in what is being said. A slightly higher-pitched and emphatic tone says, "I'm enthusiastic." A low-pitched voice conveys sadness or disappointment. Correctly using your voice requires a clear understanding of the mechanics, implications, and benefits of vocal inflection.

Make Your Voice Interesting

A monotone, lifeless voice sounds dull and unconvincing, prompting TV viewers to look for a *Seinfeld* rerun. If you want people to be interested in your messages, you must sound interesting while delivering them. In media interviews, you want your messages to stand out and be evident. Vocal inflection gives listeners an indication that what you're saying is important and interesting. It helps establish a viewpoint and adds energy and emotion to your words.

Vocal inflection is the alteration between highs and lows in pitch or tone of your voice. For both psychological and physiological reasons, facial expressions greatly affect inflection. For example, when you smile your voice naturally becomes more pleasing because the soft palate rises, making sound waves more fluid. Generally speaking, the wider you open your mouth and the more teeth you show, the better tone you get. In many cases, it's better to start an answer or statement with a low voice so you have room to raise your pitch (energy) when needed to emphasize a point or accentuate an emotion. Your inflection and range of intonation can be greatly increased by breathing properly, as described earlier in this chapter. Your vocal cords tighten when taking short breaths, but they relax and become more flexible with slow, deep breaths.

Say It Like You Mean It

Emphasizing individual words or clusters of words by speaking louder, softer, higher, or lower can dramatically change the meaning of a message. For example, consider how emphasizing certain words in the following message, as represented by the italics, alters the meaning. To get the full effect, try saying each message out loud as you read it:

Emphasis and Meaning

"*Of course* we feel bad about the spill."	This implies people presume you do not feel bad about the spill. It could come across as arrogant or patronizing.
"Of course *we* feel bad about the spill."	This suggests you are either the only one who feels bad about the spill or that others don't believe you feel bad.
"Of course we *feel bad* about the spill."	This emphasizes your concern and reveals a sense of responsibility and regret.
"Of course we feel bad about *the spill*."	This distances you from responsibility by highlighting the lack of a possessive pronoun (*the* spill vs. *our* spill).

In some circumstances, you may want to emphasize the person you're addressing. In others, you may want to emphasize yourself, your organization, or the situation at hand. In a tragedy, you'll likely want to emphasize stakeholders or victims as you present your message. To identify the appropriate emphasis in a sentence, repeat your message aloud to see how its meaning changes as you stress different words or phrases.

When Tone Falls Flat

If your company is responsible for a massive car recall and you say, "Of course we feel bad about the recall," there is ambiguity in the way the quote could be perceived. If the quote is delivered in a genuine and heartfelt manner on TV or radio, then viewers and listeners will hear the sincerity in your tone. Using the correct tone helps if people can actually hear you speak, but the effect could be skewed if your words appear in print. The message could then be perceived as cold, dismissive, and even arrogant. "Of course we feel bad about the recall," snapped Ansell. When speaking to print media, it's better to avoid phrases or words like "of course" and "obviously." Instead of saying, "Of course, we're concerned," or "Obviously we're concerned," just say, "We're concerned."

To help master vocal inflection and modulation, practice by repeating messages while looking in the mirror to see how different facial expressions affect your tone. Then try recording your voice for at least two minutes while still looking in the mirror. Play back the recording to hear how you sound to others and to track how different facial expressions and gestures affect your inflection or change the emphasis on certain words in your message. This will help you synchronize your facial expressions, body language, tone, and inflection, as well as provide the opportunity to practice proper breathing techniques.

Optimizing Message Delivery

Imagine preparing for an important media encounter—possibly a career-changing interview with the *Wall Street Journal* or a news conference to launch a groundbreaking product line. Much is at stake, so you've blocked out your three fact messages, created correlating color messages, and even come up with a clever analogy to illustrate your key concept. You've polished your presentation skills, and at least in the mirror, you look confident and comfortable. By all accounts, you're ready to face the lights, cameras, and microphones.

But wait. The reality is that no matter how well prepared you are, you cannot control every aspect of a media encounter. A news conference or an interview is a fluid situation. Formats change, reporters ask the wrong questions, and unexpected events spoil all your careful preparation. When much is at stake, there are a few critical things you should and shouldn't do in order to ensure ultimate success in communicating your messages.

What to Do

Unfortunately, there's no guaranteed formula for a successful interview or news conference. There are, however, three things you can do to ensure your messages are conveyed clearly and effectively.

- Say your messages aloud before presenting them.
- Use your messages in your answers.
- When asked if you have anything to add, answer yes.

Say Your Messages Aloud.   Once messages are created, say them out loud to make certain they sound conversational. The written word doesn't always translate into the spoken word, so spokespeople must be comfortable saying the messages aloud.

This is especially important if someone else has written the messages for you. If written with an unusual syntax or unfamiliar words, the messages will sound forced and disingenuous. If you're the one writing the messages for others, keep them short, punchy, and quotable.

Use Your Messages in Your Answers.   During a press conference, Henry Kissinger famously joked, "Does anybody have any questions for my answers?"[5] It's a witty statement, but unfortunately novice newsmakers often do wait for the right questions to be asked in order to deliver the messages that match. But sometimes the right question never comes and their messages fail to get reported in the media. If you want to see your messages on tonight's news or in tomorrow's paper, it doesn't happen by telepathy, or as my kids used to say, by ESPN. For example, if your message is to bring attention to statewide health care concerns, consider the following two possible answers:

Question: How many members are in the Health Care Association?
Answer: The Health Care Association has ten thousand members.

Compare that with:

Question: How many members are in the Health Care Association?
Answer: The Health Care Association has ten thousand members who worry about health care in the state. The problem is, statewide resources are stretched to the limit. Too many vulnerable people, including the elderly, slip through the health care cracks.

If reporters or an interviewer continually ask questions that stray from your intended message, then answer the question that is asked and look for a way to bring the answer back to your message. To do so, use conjunctives or phrases like "actually," "in fact," "the truth is," "the problem is," "what's most important," and "from my perspective." These types of phrases are commonly called "bridges" in interview or public relations jargon. If overused, "bridging" can make a spokesperson or news-maker appear evasive. However, if used in moderation, bridging can be an effective means of steering a question back to your message. For example:

Question: Tell me about today's announcement.
Answer: We're expanding our manufacturing facility by seventy-five thousand square feet and along the way we'll hire another three hundred employees. We're very optimistic about the future.
Question: But what about concerns involving poor labor-man-agement relations?
Answer: Our employees are dedicated and hardworking. *In fact,* we plan to hire three hundred more people to help us build the company. This new seventy-five-thousand square foot facility is great news for the community.

Incidentally, just because a spokesperson delivers a message, the journalist is under no obligation to quote it directly. Journalists always have the option to simply paraphrase a spokes-person's comments. That is why it is so important to craft mes-sages that can survive the media editing process.

Anything to Add? Say Yes.   When reporters ask if you have anything else you would like to add, it is not a trick question. Perhaps the reporter is concerned that he may have forgotten to ask an important question, or maybe he simply ran out of ques-tions to ask. Interviewees should see the question as free dessert, because it provides an opportunity to deliver unused messages or to reiterate important messages. Asking interviewees if they have anything to add is also of benefit to reporters who write and file stories in a hurry. Because they may not have time to listen to a recording of the entire interview, a good sound bite that wraps up the encounter is likely to be quoted.

There is a caveat, however. Though the question is not designed to entrap spokespeople, it can potentially lead to a fishing expedition. This may be the case if the interview is over and the reporter failed to dig up anything particularly newsworthy. Or the reporter may have discovered that the story she came to cover isn't really there. As journalists like to say, "Another good story spoiled by the facts." For the spokesperson, the risk is he will wander off into unprepared ground and unintentionally give the reporter a whole new story. This can become even more problematic if the spokesperson has begun to relax and likes to talk. So remember, everything you say is on the record.

What Not to Do

Executives, spokespeople, and other newsmakers trapped in the media spotlight do not instinctively know the right way to answer challenging or flustering questions from reporters. Following are three common mistakes that are certain to undermine your intended messages and ruin an opportunity to persuade stakeholders.

- Doing a brain dump
- Repeating negatives
- Starting answers with the phrases "It's true," "That's a good question," and "The answer is complex"

Don't Do a Brain Dump. John Kerry's need to deliver every message at once detracted from his 2004 presidential campaign. At a campaign stop in Albuquerque, New Mexico, retired engineer Bob Kirkpatrick asked Kerry for his views on the Israeli-Palestinian conflict. To be fair, Kirkpatrick did finally receive an answer to his question. But first, the Democratic presidential candidate said that Republican attacks on his military record were "really . . . an attack on the American people." Which Kerry then compared to President Bush's "attack on overtime." Which somehow had something to do with "settling for jobs that pay $9,000 or less." Which, in turn, was connected to the outsourcing of jobs overseas. Then Kerry shifted to the problem of weak workplace safety rules, which were "attacks" on environmental rules. Kerry finally ended by saying he would do more than the Bush administration to facilitate Middle East peace negotiations.

Kerry's brain dump unleashed a riff on Vietnam, overtime, outsourcing, worker safety, and the environment before ending up at the Middle East. No wonder the public is jaded by politicians who do not answer questions. "I sensed it was an issue he wanted to avoid," Kirkpatrick said afterward. Not surprisingly, he left the campaign stop unsure of how he would vote.[6]

Don't Repeat Negative Words. News stories with negative or inflammatory words achieve greater prominence. Furthermore, media spokespeople who use negative words can sound hotheaded and defensive, as if they have something to hide. The repetition of negative words makes already-suspect newsmakers look even more culpable. Executives and spokespeople reinforce inappropriate perceptions by answering questions with negative words. Suppose a reporter asks, "Are you incompetent?" The natural answer is, "I am not incompetent." But by answering in a way that acknowledges the issue of incompetence, the spokesperson has accepted the premise of a negative question and given it a sense of validity.

Getting newsmakers to use negative words in their answers is surprisingly easy. People get flustered by questions with negative words and do not instinctively know how to respond, so they try to create extra time to think by repeating the question. For example, a reporter may ask, "Did your previous CEO commit fraud against the company?" Put on the spot, the spokesperson responds, "Did my previous CEO commit fraud against the company? Uh, no, the previous CEO acted with integrity in all his activities." In this case, thinking out loud led the newsmaker to repeat the words "CEO" and "fraud" in the same sentence.

To make the point about the impact of negative words, communications consultant Lou Hampton has clients draw a line down the center of a blank page. On the right side of the line, he asks them to list the following terms:

Negative Word Impact

A crook
Polluting
Destroying
Gouging
Hiding
Hurting
Ignoring
Stealing
Lying
Killing

Hampton then asks people to put the word "not" to the left of the line before each of the terms, so that it now reads:

Negative Word Impact 2

Not | A crook
Not | Polluting
Not | Destroying
Not | Gouging
Not | Hiding
Not | Hurting
Not | Ignoring
Not | Stealing
Not | Lying
Not | Killing

Words like "destroying" or "gouging" certainly do not help sell a product, but are they really so bad to use? After all, the quotes say, "not destroying" and "not gouging." The fact that a business or organization is "not destroying" the environment seems like positive news. Unfortunately, the word "not" is of little help in countering the impact of negative words like polluting or destroying. Hampton points to brain-imaging research from UCLA Medical School that found the adult mind takes 50 percent longer to recognize the presence of the word "not" because the mind first creates a mental picture of vivid negative terms like crook, polluting, destroying, and gouging.[7]

This is not to suggest, however, that negative words must never be used. Some media advisers believe negative words are to be avoided at all costs, but when the news truly is bad—the CEO did commit fraud or the ship's captain was intoxicated—anything less than the truth, however negative, sounds like a cover-up.

How Not to Start Your Answers. When caught in the glare of intense media focus, many novice newsmakers resort to using standard phrases and answers. Be very careful, though, when starting an answer with any of the following three phrases:

- It's true.
- That's a good question.
- The answer is complex.

Depending on how the reporter leads into the quote, the words "It's true" could be very troublesome. For example: "Is it true that your chief financial officer lied to the Securities and Exchange Commission?" If the newsmaker responds, "It's true that our chief financial officer respects SEC rules and regulations," the reporter could use the question in a story and cut or edit the spokesperson after saying, "It's true." Ever pay attention to how the CBS program *60 Minutes* begins? Up on the screen pops a stopwatch—*tick, tick, tick*—accompanied by the voice of one of its hosts asking a question like "Is it true your chief financial officer lied to the Securities and Exchange Commission?" Then the screen cuts to a fidgeting spokesperson saying, "It's true . . ." (*tick, tick, tick*). With just this one simple edit, the exchange leaves viewers believing the company violated SEC guidelines. Sure, cutting the quote after "It's true" smacks of out-of-context reporting, but remember, it all comes down to the edit.

Many spokespeople wonder if it is appropriate to tell a reporter, "That's a good question." Depending on where the spokesperson placed the emphasis, the statement meant one of two things to me when I was a reporter. If the spokesperson said, "*That's* a good question," I would get the impression she wanted me to ask the question. That would make me feel manipulated and often lead me to work even harder to find a difficult or challenging question. If the spokesperson said, "That's a *good* question," and drew the words out, my impression would be that she was stumped. Which means, as a reporter, I would be determined to pursue that line of questioning. Either way, the outcome would most likely be negative for the spokesperson.

Likewise, when reporters hear spokespeople say, "The answer is complex," they interpret it one of two ways. Either the spokesperson thinks the reporter is too stupid to understand the answer or the spokesperson doesn't have a clue how to answer and wants to hide behind the excuse that it's too complex. It's always better not to use the word "complex" in explaining an issue or answer. It is a spokesperson's job to make complex issues simple and easy for stakeholders to digest. That, in a nutshell, is what well-crafted messages are for.

Messages as Mantra

As mentioned at the beginning of the previous chapter, a study published in the *Journal of Personality and Social Psychology* discovered that "the more an opinion has been encountered in the past, the more accessible it is in memory and the more familiar it seems when it is encountered again."[8] Clearly, the more times individuals hear an opinion, the more comfort they develop with what they're hearing. But does that mean spokespeople should be relentless in their reiteration of a message? Absolutely not. The key to effectively communicating your messages to the media is to find the balance between being responsive to questions journalists ask and putting forth what you want the media to report.

Some executives, politicians, and spokespeople believe the secret to a successful media interview is to pay no attention to questions and simply repeat their messages, regardless of what they are asked. Take the case of former Toronto mayor Mel Lastman. Lastman was known for speaking his mind and sometimes sounding silly in the process. On an overseas visit to pitch Toronto as an Olympic host, Lastman was asked whether his international tour would take him to Africa. Having seen one too many Bob Hope and Bing Crosby movies, Lastman responded that he was afraid to go to Africa for fear of being eaten by cannibals. "Why the hell do I want to go to Mombassa?" he asked. "I'm sort of scared about going there. I just see myself in a pot of boiling water with all these natives dancing around me." Predictably, community leaders immediately rebuked the mayor for what they considered racist comments against people of African origin. To address the controversy, Lastman wanted all to know he was sorry, but the way he delivered that message made the situation worse. The following exchange between reporters and the mayor highlights the downside of ignoring questions and simply repeating your messages:

> *Reporter:* Do you think you should resign?
> *Lastman:* I am truly sorry that I made the remarks. I'm sorry that I made the remarks.
> *Reporter:* Is "sorry" enough?

Lastman: I'm sorry I made the remarks.

Reporter: How much damage do you think you did to the Olympic bid?

Lastman: I'm sorry I made the remarks. My comments were inappropriate.

Reporter: That's not what I asked.

Lastman: That's my answer.

Reporter: How much damage have you done to the city?

Lastman: I'm truly sorry.

Reporter: Are you considering resigning?

Lastman: I'm truly sorry that I made those remarks.

Reporter: Are you considering resigning as a result of making those remarks?

Lastman: I'm truly sorry that I made those remarks.

Reporter: Are you considering resigning?

Lastman: I'm truly sorry.

Reporter: What are you going to do around damage control?

Lastman: I'm truly sorry I made the remarks. My comments were inappropriate.

Reporter: Are you going to Europe to lobby for the bid as planned?

Lastman: I'm very sorry about the remarks.

Reporter: Are you sorry about the remarks you made?

Lastman: Yes. Yes, I am.

Reporter: Why did you make them?

Lastman: I'm sorry I made the remarks and my comments were completely inappropriate and I want to apologize to anybody who's offended.

Reporter: Why did you say them?

Lastman: It was just the wrong thing to say and I'm sorry I made them. I mean, what do you want from me except I'm sorry? I did the wrong thing.

Reporter: Did you goof?

Lastman: Of course I did. That's why I'm apologizing.

Reporter: Why did you make them?

Lastman: I'm sorry I made the remarks.

Reporter: What can you do to make amends?

Lastman: I'm sorry I made the remarks.

Reporter: Are you a racist?

Lastman: I'm sorry I made the remarks and I'm sorry, again sorry, that my comments were inappropriate and I again apologize to anyone that is offended by my comments.[9]

Mercifully, Mayor Lastman's advisers, who no doubt had told him to repeatedly say "I'm sorry," then stepped in to attempt a rescue. Clearly, the mayor needed a message. "I'm sorry" is effective enough, only its recitation eighteen times cheapened its sincerity, especially for those who viewed the entire exchange.

The message as mantra is a manipulative tactic to put forward responses that have no correlation to the questions asked. Many times I hear PR professionals tell spokespeople to be positive and repeat their message regardless of what they are asked. Evasion of this sort breeds distrust and damages credibility. Spokespeople who simply regurgitate their messages ad nauseam are perceived as unresponsive and less trustworthy. And in the end, the messages they have worked so hard to convey fail to convince stakeholders.

Same Message, Different Words

Spokespeople concerned about the repetition of a message can vary the words. Instead of repeating the same message three times, find three different ways to make the same point. For example:

- Our new product will revolutionize the world of personal computers.
- We're transforming the world of personal computers into a new and electrifying experience.
- How people see and use their personal computers will never be the same.

Though the words differ, the messaging theme is consistent.

Message Delivery Development

By this point, you may be wondering how the novice spokesperson or busy executive is supposed to remember all this information while standing in front of an audience or struggling through questions from reporters. With experience, all of these techniques and strategies become easier to implement. To assist spokespeople and newsmakers in need of immediate help, however, I recommend focusing on what I consider the five key behaviors of successful message delivery:

1. Breathe.
2. Pause.
3. Talk with your hands.
4. Make eye contact.
5. Say your messages aloud.

Of course, knowing what you should do and actually being able to do it are two completely different things. After all, what's the good of knowing that you should pause between ideas if you forget to do so as soon as the cameras start rolling? Following are a few simple activities designed to help you incorporate these essential behaviors into presentations, interviews, and news conferences.

Practice, Practice, Practice

All good spokespeople have one trait in common—they practice. Like a professional basketball player draining extra jump shots or a surgeon training to perform a complicated procedure, spokespeople must practice basic presentation skills in order to communicate with confidence and credibility.

One of the best ways to practice breathing properly is to establish a system of constant reminders. For example, write "breathe" on a notecard and put it in your shirt pocket. Then, every time you retrieve something from your pocket you'll be reminded to breathe properly. Likewise, put a sticky note on your alarm clock. Then, the first thing you'll see every morning is a reminder to breathe. After you turn off your alarm, take five minutes to practice breathing. You'll be surprised how proper breathing can help reduce tension and anxiety at the beginning of your day. There are very few situations as stressful as being stuck in heavy traffic, especially when you have appointments to keep. Consider placing a note on your dashboard reminding you to breathe. This will acclimate your body to breathing properly in stressful situations. It's also helpful to post signs or notes in your office, at home, and especially on your desk near the phone. When you deliver an important presentation, be sure to post a sticky note on the lectern or write "breathe" at the top of your notes. If you're concerned about reporters seeing the note, just write the letter B. All of these small actions will help you develop the muscle memory necessary to keep breathing even under the most difficult circumstances.

To practice pausing, talking with your hands, and making eye contact, take advantage of social situations like dinner parties, get-togethers, and family reunions. All of these events are opportunities to observe natural communication behaviors and practice effective delivery skills. As you circulate or mingle, work on listening and making eye contact. When you do say something, be sure to pause in order to ensure your comments register. If you have the chance to address a cluster of people, be sure to deliver one thought to one face. Then, shift your eyes to make contact with another person as you continue to speak. Pay close attention to other people's hand gestures during normal conversation and observe how their movements change depending on the tone of the discussion. Try experimenting with different gestures during a conversation and create a mental catalogue of a few movements that seem particularly effective or comfortable. Although these and other social exchanges provide opportunities to refine individual communication skills, one of the best ways to develop a comprehensive understanding of successful messaging behaviors is to perform the following exercise before an important interview or presentation.

Message Delivery Exercise

Although relatively simple, this powerful five-step exercise will help you become more familiar with your message content, feel more in control of your environment, and reduce excessive nervousness and anxiety. For the best results, try to perform the exercise in front of a colleague, friend, or family member. If no one is available to help, do it in front of a mirror.

Step 1: Say Your Message(s) Aloud. As mentioned earlier, the spoken word is very different from the written word. Reading your messages aloud ensures they sound conversational. Stand up so you feel more exposed and vulnerable. Do your messages convey the ideas, concepts, and themes you hope to project? Do they roll off the tongue and sound natural to the ear?

Step 2: Say Your Message(s) Aloud and Focus on Breathing Properly. Now reread your messages and work on breathing properly. Take slow, deep breaths:

Breathe in: Belly out.
Breathe out: Belly in.

If you have trouble remembering to breathe, write the word "breathe" or the letter B on your message sheet or note cards.

Step 3: Say Your Message(s) Aloud and Focus on Breathing Properly and Pausing between Thoughts. As you read through your messages a third time, begin layering the habits. Remember to breathe, but now pause after every significant idea. This is particularly important for ideas or messages you hope to emphasize. What do you want your audience to take away from your message? If you find it difficult to pause, write "pause" or "slow down" on your notes.

Step 4: Say Your Message(s) Aloud and Focus on Breathing Properly, Pausing between Thoughts, and Using Your Hands. Follow the same process as above but now remember to use strong, deliberate hand gestures. Do your hands match the rhythm and meaning of your words? If not, you may need to adjust the tone of your voice to match the strength and conviction of your hands.

Step 5: Say Your Message(s) Aloud and Focus on Breathing Properly, Pausing between Thoughts, Using Your Hands, and Making Strong Eye Contact. By this point, you should be familiar enough with your messages to recite them from memory. Also, your breathing should be comfortable and you should have well-timed pauses. While establishing eye contact, remember to direct one thought to one face. Practice shifting your eyes to engage the entire audience. If you're practicing in front of one person, pick other points in the room to represent different parts of the audience.

If you identify flaws or weak points in your presentation, repeat the appropriate exercise steps to address those weaknesses. A few extra minutes of preparation can significantly increase your aptitude. And remember, if you ever feel overwhelmed or flustered while delivering your messages, recalibrate by breathing and pausing.

Biojax Part 5: Message Delivery Skills in Practice

When we first met Joan Smith in Chapter One, she was aggressively questioned about the price of her company's new biological therapy, Biojax. Even though she was convinced she had a positive story to tell, she was upset by the resulting news report. In fact, her initial comment was "You took me out of context. Where's the rest of what I said?" In subsequent chapters, Joan utilized a collection of messaging tools—the Value Compass, the Problem Solution Formula template, and the Compelling Message Creator—to prepare for an interview do-over in Chapter Six. The final step in preparing for this new interview is for Joan to practice presenting her messages. To do so, I ran her through the preceding five-step message delivery exercise. During the exercise, I used a few special techniques to help her correct flaws and weaknesses in her presentation style. These are all simple techniques that any colleague, family member, or friend can use to help you as you prepare for an important interview or presentation.

For the exercise, Joan and I used a normal conference room containing an oval table and eight chairs. To start, I asked Joan to stand at the front of the conference room and read through the messages she had prepared with the Compelling Message Creator.

Gamely, Joan read through her entire message sheet. I immediately noticed a number of issues. First, she clutched her hands uncomfortably in front of her. Then, as she read through the messages, her voice was monotone and her expression was blank. Also, she repeatedly said "uh" as a way to link ideas, and instead of making direct eye contact, her eyes would wander around the room. Frankly, it was uncomfortable to watch.

Once Joan was done, she asked how she did.

"It's a start," I said, smiling.

We talked about the importance of breathing properly and reviewed the correct way to breathe. "Breathing is the operating system for good communication," I told her. I suggested she write "breathe" at the top of her message sheet. Then I asked her to read through her messages again.

This time, breathing properly helped her slow down a bit and she certainly was better at repeating her messages. However, she still clutched her hands, looked uncomfortable, and linked thoughts with the word "uh."

Once she finished, I said, "You're doing great." Then I asked her to read through the messages again, but this time trying to pause after each thought or idea. "To help you," I explained, "I'll hold up my hand if you're talking too fast or you need to pause to let an idea sink in, okay?"

Joan nodded.

"Also, you have a bad habit of saying 'uh' between thoughts or messages."

"I know, but I can't help it," she acknowledged.

"It's okay. To help you break the habit, I'll clap each time you do it." I demonstrated by clapping my hands together once.

After a couple of deep breaths, Joan started repeating her messages. She was clearly focused on breathing and trying not to say "uh." I only needed to clap twice during the entire reading. When she started speaking too fast or she needed to pause, I held up my hand. But by the end of her messages, she was consciously talking slower and pausing after each main idea.

"Much, much better," I said when she'd finished.

Joan smiled. "It's hard to talk and think about all these things at the same time."

"It's good that it's hard. It means you're trying. Now let's do it again. Only this time, instead of bunching up your hands in front of you, I want you to gesture and use your hands naturally. Like I'm doing right now," I said, gesturing with my hands as I talked. "Okay?"

"Sure," Joan said. She repositioned herself at the front of the room and held out her hands. She seemed ready to start, but then she looked at me. "What should I do with them?"

"Try holding them about chest high and a little farther apart than your shoulders. Now curl and separate your fingers slightly. Like this." I demonstrated what I meant.

Joan mirrored my movements.

"Once you begin speaking," I added, "let your hand movements follow along naturally. And remember, use strong, deliberate movements. No limp or weak hands, all right?"

Joan started reciting her messages again. By this point, she no longer needed her message sheet. About halfway through, though, I stopped her.

"What's wrong?"

"Your hands. You're not really moving them; you're just wiggling your fingers."

Joan frowned. "I don't feel right making bold gestures."

"Not every gesture needs to be bold. Some can be conciliatory, some can illustrate enthusiasm. Your tone needs to match your hands and your hands need to match your tone. They need to synchronize. In some cases that may mean you need to strengthen your voice and vary your tone to match your gestures. In other cases, you may need to strengthen your gestures to match your voice. In this case, you have important messages to convey. People's lives are at stake and strong emotions are involved. Say your messages with conviction and let your hands help animate the importance and the emotions of your words."

"Got it," Joan said. She refocused and started from the beginning. Her breathing was consistent. I clapped once when she said "uh" and I had to slow her down a couple of times, but soon she was emphasizing important words and becoming more animated as she talked. She no longer sounded like she was reading notes or delivering calculated sound bites. Instead, her words and movements reflected a true conviction in her messages and a heartfelt concern for her stakeholders.

When she finished, I said, "That was fantastic."

"It *was* good, wasn't it?"

"It was great, but let's do it again."

Joan groaned.

"Just one more time," I assured her. I asked her to return to the front of the room. I told her I would still clap or hold up my hand if needed, but now I would add one more signal to help her with making eye contact and engaging the entire audience.

"What audience?" she asked, laughing.

Since we were the only two people in the conference room, I told her I would point to empty chairs around the table to indicate where she should look. "Start by looking at me, then I'll point there or there or there. Once I point, finish your thought or idea before looking to the next part of the audience. Remember, one thought, one face. Are you ready?"

Joan took a couple of deep breaths and started from the top. Now her breathing was natural, her pauses well-timed, and her hands more animated. At first, she was a little awkward in changing eye-lines, but she soon found a comfortable rhythm for finishing ideas, pausing, and engaging different parts of the room.

When she finished, I couldn't help but smile. The improvement was nothing short of extraordinary. I must admit, however, I wasn't completely surprised. I've seen similar results with thousands of students and clients. What is surprising is that such a simple exercise can produce such dramatic change. As I mentioned earlier, you can do this exact same exercise at home or in the office. Just ask another person to observe you and provide the necessary signals to help you alter bad habits and refine your presentation skills. If you, like Joan, take the time to identify and correct your weaknesses, you'll be amazed at how effectively you can engage stakeholders.

Chapter Talking Points

- Remember to breathe deeply and speak slowly.
- Use your hands while talking to look natural and help release anxiety.
- Avoid body language leakage—those involuntary movements that indicate you're nervous or stressed. In particular, avoid head nodding, swallowing, and pursing your lips.

- Make strong eye contact to ensure listeners are engaged. If addressing an audience, deliver one complete thought to one face or one part of the room before shifting eye contact.

- Use voice inflection (modulation between highs and lows in pitch) to inject energy and emotion into your messages.

- Say your messages aloud before presenting them in order to confirm that they're conversational and quotable.

- Use your messages in your answers even if reporters fail to ask the right questions or stray from your intended subject.

- Avoid repeating negative words that reporters use in questions. Doing so indicates that you accept the negative premise.

- If you ever feel overwhelmed while being interviewed or speaking in front of an audience, recalibrate by breathing and pausing.

6

WHEN THE GOING GETS TOUGH

"Scandal or controversy beats ordinary reporting hands down."

—*Tony Blair, former Prime Minister of Britain*

Unemployment. Divorce. Illness. Throughout life, unexpected and challenging events occur. Not every situation can be planned for and managed. Many of these unpredictable and unexpected circumstances offer the potential for error, failure, even tragedy. Dealing with the media is no different. When the headline is you, every day can be a new adventure or a new disaster. Concerned with finding the story and finding it first, reporters have little reluctance in asking antagonistic or intentionally misleading questions. If necessary, they'll resort to embarrassing silences, dogged questioning, and ambush tactics in order to secure the quotes they need. Spokespeople and newsmakers can manage these difficult circumstances in one of two ways: they can handle them poorly, in which case events will worsen and often spiral into a full-blown public relations crisis, or they can manage them well, in which case negative media exposure will be reduced and public relations damage will be minimal. Successfully navigating the most difficult and demanding media confrontations requires being mindful of the fact that unforeseen challenges exist in nearly every media interaction, and having specific strategies to deal with these challenges. In this chapter, I will examine some of the most difficult situations encountered when dealing with the media and provide step-by-step strategies for effectively controlling these situations, including techniques for managing surprise encounters, hostile questioning, and relentless reporters.

Surprise Encounters

John Cleghorn, chairman, CEO, and president of RBC, Canada's largest bank, was leaving a luncheon when he was confronted by an elderly woman named Betty Hyde. Like other banks across North America, RBC was closing branches because many customers had switched to using ATMs and online banking, but Mrs. Hyde wanted Cleghorn to keep her branch in Ottawa open. Mrs. Hyde argued that most seniors are without computers and weekly visits to the bank represent an outing for many of them. Taking the bank branch away was going to hurt people, Mrs. Hyde claimed.

As Cleghorn left the luncheon hall, he saw Mrs. Hyde approach him accompanied by a TV camera sent by a national consumer show. When Mrs. Hyde began to explain the problem, Cleghorn, all six-feet-plus of him, became defensive. He stood there arguing with an elderly woman who looked as if she had just come from baking cookies. The good-versus-evil visuals were classic. Cleghorn might as well have smashed his car into a station wagon full of nuns. It was obvious from the start that he was not going to win the encounter. What follows is a transcript of the exchange as it unfolded on the CBC TV show *Marketplace*:

> *Betty Hyde:* I want to speak to you about some of the 15
>   percent of us who don't use electronic banking.
> *John Cleghorn:* Right—
> *Betty Hyde:* And five hundred of us have protested by
>   petition the proposed closure of your bank on Beechwood,
>   a neighborhood that is replete with seniors like myself
>   who value the services . . .

John Cleghorn: Mmm—

Betty Hyde: . . . of the bank and I wanted to hear what you
have to say about those services which are being
withdrawn.

John Cleghorn: Well, not that particular branch location,
madam. I'm not sure about the details. We have sixteen
hundred branches. . . .

Betty Hyde (interrupting): I have written to you twice about
this.

John Cleghorn: Well no, I know, I'm. . . . I—

At that point, the TV show cut to Betty Hyde speaking on
camera after the exchange. Clearly upset, she said that Cleghorn
told her to contact one of his vice presidents. To Mrs. Hyde,
Cleghorn's message was clear. It was, as she succinctly phrased
it, "Take that woman off my hands."[1] Cleghorn was clearly flustered. Based on what was broadcast, here is what happened to
him from the moment he was confronted:

- He stopped breathing.
- He stopped listening.
- He immediately began thinking, "How am I going
  to answer?"
- He began to argue.

To be fair, most people caught in this situation would likely
have reacted in a similar manner. But there is a better way.
When caught off-guard in a surprise encounter, follow this series
of steps:

Step 1: Breathe.

Step 2: Listen.

Step 3: Stop thinking about what to say—just listen.

Step 4: Ask questions to ensure you understand the problem.

Step 5: Repeat the concerns you just heard to show that you truly are listening.

Step 6: Ask the person whether your summary of the situation is accurate. If they say "no," then tell them it's important to you to get it right, and ask them to repeat their concerns.

Step 7: If you still don't know what to say, then at least deliver a message that reflects your concern, such as, "I can see how much this situation troubles you."

Angry, upset people want two things from you. The first thing they want is for you to acknowledge their problem. The second thing they want is for you to solve the problem, which is not always possible while standing in a hallway or a parking lot. Unless Cleghorn was prepared to set company policy on the fly, which is rarely a good idea, how could he have ended the encounter with his credibility and dignity intact? He could have tapped into the concern and emotion inherent in the moment and invoked his Value Compass. Cleghorn could have said, "Ma'am, it's clear this is important to you. When I get back to my office I will immediately look into this situation. Mrs. Hyde, will you be home at three o'clock this afternoon? May I please call you then to bring you up to date? Ma'am, what's your phone number?"

Then, rather than have an assistant write down the number, Cleghorn should have taken the number himself, either on a piece of paper or on his smartphone. The visual of the president of Canada's largest bank writing down the number of an elderly customer would have shown how much he cared and likely been the defining image of the encounter. By the way, after this encounter Cleghorn kept the RBC branch open for six months— and then, when no one was looking, he closed it.

When the Problem Is Bigger Than You

Organizations in both the private and public sectors often struggle with widespread issues like health care, education, energy, crime, and social injustice. Many of these are systemic problems unlikely to be solved by a single company or organization. Instead, they require significant social change or sweeping public initiatives. In addition, some issues are inherent to specific industries or sectors. Consider the many legacy costs and developmental challenges faced by the auto industry, airline industry, and public utilities. When dealing with bad news problems that are bigger than your individual company or organization, consider using the Share the Blame Formula.

The Share the Blame Formula

This formula is a first cousin of the Problem Solution Formula in that it is made up of two clauses or phrases joined by a conjunction. The first half of the sentence spreads the blame by identifying a prevalent or systemic problem, while the second half of the sentence takes credit for the solution. For example, the 2004 SARS outbreak in Toronto affected almost every business in the city. People were quarantined, businesses lost money, and tourism ground to a virtual halt. Companies were lying low, waiting for the disease to run its course. A retail executive interviewed about the impact of SARS could use the Share the Blame Formula to say, "Business for all companies has been impacted by SARS, and our plan is to provide consumers with significant incentives to shop with us at this time." With this response, the retailer both identifies the communal nature of the problem (business is down for everyone) and presents a plan for addressing it (increasing incentives to bring in customers).

Another example of the Share the Blame Formula involves a public utility experiencing a fire in an electric vault that takes out power in the downtown core. Obviously, individuals and businesses would be frustrated, inconvenienced, and even economically affected. Most likely they would blame the utility, but the problem is largely due to the antiquated infrastructure of the nationwide electrical grid. In this case, an effective Share the Blame Formula message would be the following: "Utilities across North America are grappling with an aging infrastructure, and that's why we're investing millions of dollars to upgrade the vault network in our community."

Assuring the Blame Is Shared

The creation of a Share the Blame Formula message is tricky because once it is edited it may still look like your problem. Say your company is building a new sports stadium funded by public money and there is widespread concern because the project is over budget. Consider this possible Share the Blame Formula message: "Keeping on budget is a challenge for every major construction project and we're doing our very best to manage costs." Sounds good, but this quote was structured in a manner that did not successfully spread the blame. A reporter could simply quote the beginning of the message, "Keeping on budget is a challenge," which has you owning a problem that others own as well. Now, compare that message to this one: "Construction projects of this size in cities everywhere face budget challenges and we're doing our best to manage costs." By inserting the words "in cities everywhere" between "construction projects of this size" and "face budget challenges," it becomes very difficult for a reporter to edit out the shared failure and make it only your problem.

A word of caution, however, about Share the Blame Formula messages. Even though your company experiences some problems that could just as easily happen to others, be careful not to use the Share the Blame Formula if it sounds like an excuse. If, for example, your car company is recalling hundreds of thousands of vehicles because of a fuel injection problem, it is not appropriate to say, "At some point, almost every vehicle manufacturer is in a recall situation and we've designed a plan to correct the fuel injection problem." The fact is those other vehicle manufacturers have not recalled their cars because of faulty fuel injectors, but your company has. The problem is yours and you need to own it.

When You Say Something Stupid

In the previous chapter, I introduced the story of former Toronto mayor Mel Lastman. Lastman, known for speaking his mind, embarrassed himself and the city of Toronto by joking that he was afraid of being eaten by cannibals while visiting Africa. As a journalist, I interviewed Mel Lastman many times and am convinced the impact of his comment did not match his intent. Ill-advised as it was, the mayor foolishly made the remark in jest, without considering possible consequences. The controversy fueled local feelings of outrage and triggered cries across the city for Mayor Lastman to resign. At a news conference, he attempted to apologize for his remarks, but failed miserably. While you can find a more complete transcript of his disastrous apology in Chapter Five, it will be helpful to reexamine the most difficult portion of the incident:

> *Lastman:* I'm sorry I made the remarks and my comments were completely inappropriate and I want to apologize to anybody who's offended.
>
> *Reporter:* Why did you say them?
>
> *Lastman:* It was just the wrong thing to say and I'm sorry I made them. I mean, what do you want from me except I'm sorry? I did the wrong thing.
>
> *Reporter:* Did you goof?
>
> *Lastman:* Of course I did. That's why I'm apologizing.
>
> *Reporter:* Why did you make them?

Lastman: I'm sorry I made the remarks.

Reporter: What can you do to make amends?

Lastman: I'm sorry I made the remarks.

Reporter: Are you a racist?

Lastman: _____

The question of whether Mayor Lastman is a racist is certainly hard-hitting. It's the type of question that can fluster even the most experienced spokesperson or newsmaker. Here is how the mayor actually answered the question when it was asked: "I'm sorry I made the remarks and I'm sorry, again sorry, that my comments were inappropriate and I again apologize to anyone that is offended by my comments."[2]

It is likely the mayor's aides rehearsed that question with him prior to the news conference, but the response he delivered was blatantly evasive. So what were the mayor's response options to the question of racism? Following are the four most likely approaches:

- "No, I am not a racist." (negative)
- "Yes, I am a racist." (not true and unlikely to be said)
- "I won't dignify that question with a response." (sounds defensive)
- "No comment." (the equivalent of "I'm hiding something.")

Clearly, none of these are good options. Each leads to a negative interpretation, more intensive questioning, or an extended news cycle. So what should you say when a question flusters you or when any answer you give will work against you?

The Fluster Strategy

To be fair, newsmakers and spokespeople cannot be expected to always know the right thing to say. The Fluster Strategy is the tool to use when you are, figuratively speaking, trapped in a burning hallway and you can't find the exit door. Here are the four steps:

Step 1: Breathe—because you've likely stopped due to stress.

Step 2: Say, "Excuse me," or "I beg your pardon," but not with attitude. After you say it, continue breathing and stop talking. Do not let silence make you feel awkward. Make peace with silence. After all, it's not a dinner party and you're not the host.

Step 3: Once the reporter repeats the question, say, "Please help me understand the context of the question."

Step 4: After the reporter provides greater context, address the subtext of the question.

Steps One and Two of the Fluster Strategy offer an opportunity to regain composure and synchronize your brain and tongue. Step Three compels the reporter to peel away layers of the question. In so doing, the reporter elaborates on the intent of the question and gives the respondent additional information to work with and more time to think. For example:

Reporter: Does your CEO engage in sexual harassment?
Spokesperson (deep breath): Excuse me?"

A moment of silence while the reporter gauges the spokesperson, then:

Reporter: I asked whether your CEO engages in sexual harassment.
Spokesperson: Please help me understand the context of the question.

> *Reporter:* My question is simple enough. There are stories circulating that your CEO has sexually harassed a number of female executives. Is it true?

At this point, many spokespeople would be uncertain of how to continue. When that happens, simply move to Step Four and look to the subtext of the controversial or confrontational question to identify what lies beneath it. For instance, the assertion that the CEO engages in sexual harassment implies a lack of integrity and professionalism on his part. Now, presuming the CEO is indeed a man of integrity and the allegation is totally baseless, the respondent could answer by addressing the question's subtext:

> *Spokesperson:* Our CEO conducts himself in a professional manner and treats all people with dignity and respect.

When you are asked whether recent budget cuts have led to unsafe working conditions, what is the subtext of the question—that is, what is driving the question in the first place? The question of cutting budgets to skimp on safety implies that your company cares little for worker well-being and is largely motivated by the bottom line. With clear insight into the emotional subtext of the question, a possible response—providing you believe it to be true and can back it up—is: "Working conditions must always be safe."

Regarding the question of whether Mayor Mel Lastman is a racist, let's apply the Fluster Strategy and see the results:

> *Reporter:* Are you a racist?
> *Lastman (deep breath):* Excuse me?
> *Reporter:* I asked if you are a racist.
> *Lastman:* Please help me understand the context of the question.

Reporter: You made disparaging remarks about African people, implying they are cannibals and uncivilized. Many consider those remarks to be racist. Are you a racist?

Lastman (understanding the subtext as an implication of intolerance): Diversity is what makes this city strong. I value our city's diversity and the richness it offers all of us. Those who know me understand what's in my heart.

Although this approach does provide the spokesperson with more time and information, it doesn't always put a question or issue to rest. When a reporter persists with a specific line of questioning, you need a strategy for concluding that area of inquiry and moving the discussion forward.

The Closure Strategy

Reporters do not abandon questions easily. They ask the same questions over and over, and in the process, pull every tooth out of your mouth until you're gumming the interview. The repetitive asking of a question usually occurs for one of two reasons. First, it is possible the spokesperson is being evasive and that causes the reporter to keep pressing. When that's the case, the reporter is justified in continually asking the question. The second reason reporters grab hold of a spokesperson's pant leg and won't let go is because the spokesperson did not answer in the way the journalist hoped. Either the spokesperson did not repeat the ugly, negative words in his response or his answer did not portray him as being either the villain or the "village idiot" needed for a front-page story.

When the same question is repeatedly asked, it is your signal that the reporter is not interested in your message and that the question itself, as well as the answer you give, will form a pivotal part of the story. Often, when spokespeople are pummeled in this manner, they weaken and end up providing the one quote they were determined to avoid. In the Mel Lastman case, this was an evasive version of "I am not a racist." To avoid this fate, use the Closure Strategy to bring the line of questioning to an end. There are either three or four steps to the Closure Strategy, depending on the persistence of the reporter. Here is how the Closure Strategy works:

Step 1: The first time the question is asked, answer honestly in a way that serves your purpose and reflects your prepared message.

Step 2: The second time the question is asked, preface your response with, "As I said," and then paraphrase your message so it doesn't sound like your general counsel crafted it.

Step 3: The third time the question is asked, answer by saying, "I've answered the question a couple of times. If you like, I'll answer it one last time before we move on," and then, once again, paraphrase your message.

In Step Three, do not say you will answer the question "again" or "one more time." Use the word "last." However, avoid saying "For the last time" because it has a harsh edge to it. The phrase "one last time" indicates that you are being accommodating, but it still conveys a sense of finality. Using the Mayor Lastman news conference, here is an example of the Closure Strategy in use:

Reporter: Are you are a racist?

Lastman: Diversity is what makes this city strong. I value our city's diversity and the richness it offers all of us. Those who know me understand what's in my heart.

Reporter: You didn't answer my question. Yes or no, are you a racist?

Lastman: As I said, we can be proud of our city's diversity and all the value it offers our community.

Reporter: You are clearly being evasive—answer my question! Are you a racist?

Lastman: I've answered the question a couple of times and if you like, I'll answer it one last time before we move on. Our diversity is a source of pride for the city. Diversity is what makes this city the gem that it is.

If the journalist refuses to abandon the question and presses you a fourth time, invoke Step Four, which I call "final closure." Step Four can be used in phone interviews, one-on-one encounters, or even in gaggles where a newsmaker is surrounded by many reporters. If the question is asked a fourth time, then:

Step 4: Bring the discussion to final closure by stating, "I have time to answer this one last question and then I must move on to my next meeting. Our community is strengthened by our diversity. I'm grateful for your interest and please call on me any time I can be of service. Thanks very much. I wish you all the best. Good-bye."

While the Fluster Strategy and the Closure Strategy can be used separately, flustering questions can often develop into a tenaciously pursued line of questioning. Use the Cluster Strategy if a reporter asks a flustering question in a persistent fashion.

The Cluster Strategy

As the name indicates, the Cluster Strategy is a blend of both the Fluster Strategy and the Closure Strategy. Again, using the Mayor Lastman incident, here's an example of how it works:

Reporter: Are you a racist?

Lastman (deep breath): Excuse me?

Reporter: I asked if you are a racist.

Lastman: Please help me understand the context of the question.

Reporter: You made disparaging remarks about African people, implying they are cannibals and uncivilized. Many consider those remarks to be racist. Are you a racist?

Lastman: Diversity is what makes this city strong. I value our city's diversity and the richness it offers all of us. Those who know me understand what's in my heart.

Reporter: Yes, but are you a racist?

Lastman: As I said, we can be proud of our city's diversity and all the value it offers our community.

Reporter: You are clearly being evasive—answer my question! Are you a racist?

Lastman: I've answered the question a couple of times and if you like, I'll answer it one last time before we move on. Our diversity is a source of pride for the city. Diversity is what makes this city the gem that it is.

For your convenience, all of the preceding strategies are presented in a clear, condensed format in Exhibit 6.1. I encourage you to make a copy of the exhibit and review it before important media interactions.

Be Prepared to Sincerely Apologize

Human beings have a tremendous capacity to forgive those who acknowledge wrongdoing and apologize for harming or offending others. Therefore, when mistakes are made, it is best to own up to them. To be heartfelt and genuine, an apology must acknowledge a mistake or failure, take responsibility, state regret, and commit to behaviors and relationships going forward. The concern of many, however, is that apologies constitute admissions of guilt and therefore increase the potential for liability. Some jurisdictions in the United States consider an apology to be an admission of guilt. Therefore, lawyers fearing lawsuits usually advise clients to steer clear of apologies.

Exhibit 6.1. Strategy Summary

Surprise Encounters

When caught off-guard in a surprise encounter, follow this series of steps:

1. Breathe.
2. Listen.
3. Stop thinking about what to say—just listen.
4. Ask questions to ensure you understand the problem.
5. Repeat the concerns you just heard to show that you truly are listening.
6. Ask the person whether your summary of the situation is accurate. If they say "no," then tell them it's important to you to get it right and ask them to repeat their concerns.
7. If you still don't know what to say, then at least deliver a message that reflects your concern, such as, "I can see how much this situation troubles you."

The Fluster Strategy

When you are flustered by a reporter's question, follow these four steps:

1. Breathe—because you've likely stopped due to stress.
2. Say, "Excuse me" or "I beg your pardon," but without attitude. After you say it, continue breathing and stop talking.
3. Once the reporter repeats the question, say, "Please help me understand the context of the question."
4. After the reporter provides greater context, address the subtext or deeper implication of the question.

The Closure Strategy

There are either three or four steps to the Closure Strategy, depending on the persistence of the reporter. Here is how the Closure Strategy works:

1. The first time the question is asked, answer honestly in a way that serves your purpose and reflects your prepared message.
2. The second time the question is asked, preface your response with, "As I said," and then paraphrase your message.

3. The third time the question is asked, answer by saying, "I've answered the question a couple of times. If you like, I'll answer it one last time before we move on," and then, once again, paraphrase your message.

4. If the journalist refuses to abandon the question and presses you a fourth time, bring the discussion to final closure by stating, "I have time to answer this one last question and then I must move on to my next meeting." Paraphrase your message one last time, then state, "I'm grateful for your interest and please call on me any time I can be of service. Thanks very much. I wish you all the best. Good-bye."

The Cluster Strategy

Use the Cluster Strategy if a reporter asks a flustering question in a persistent fashion. As the name indicates, the Cluster Strategy is a blend of both the Fluster Strategy and the Closure Strategy:

1. Breathe.

2. Say, "Excuse me" or "I beg your pardon," but without attitude. After you say it, continue breathing and stop talking.

3. Once the reporter repeats the question, say, "Please help me understand the context of the question."

4. After the reporter provides greater context, address the subtext or the deeper implications of the question.

5. The second time the question is asked, preface your response with, "As I said," and then paraphrase your message.

6. The third time the question is asked, answer by saying, "I've answered the question a couple of times. If you like, I'll answer it one last time before we move on," and then, once again, paraphrase your message.

7. If the journalist refuses to abandon the question and presses you a fourth time, bring the discussion to final closure by stating, "I have time to answer this one last question and then I must move on to my next meeting." Paraphrase your message one last time, then state, "I'm grateful for your interest and please call on me any time I can be of service. Thanks very much. I wish you all the best. Good-bye."

For that reason, the Ontario legislature recently passed the Apology Act, to encourage more people to own up to their mistakes, without fear of their apology being used against them in court. Three Canadian provinces and thirty-five U.S. states have such a law on the books. "It has substantially reduced lawsuits and settlements and claims in the court system because people were able to have a discussion about what's taken place and bring closure to a particular issue," said Ontario legislator David Orazietti.[3] It is worth noting that in a number of U.S. states, including California, Florida, and Texas, certain types of apologies are not admissible as evidence.[4]

Once again, lawyer Jim Golden, who defends trucking companies involved in road disasters, takes a unique perspective. "There's a difference between saying I'm sorry, and it was our fault and we're legally responsible. But in a case of clear liability I encourage us not only to say we're sorry, I encourage us to say we're sorry and it was our fault. This accident would not have happened but for our negligence." What about concerns of enhanced liability resulting from such an admission? Golden isn't worried about the legal impact of saying I'm sorry: "People want to feel that justice has been done. There's a sense that if you admit you're wrong, it doesn't have to be proven in a court of law. If you do it and you're genuine about it and they can tell it's coming from your heart, as opposed to it being some sort of technique so you can manipulate someone, I think it is profoundly positive." Saying "I'm sorry" when an accident is clearly your fault helps begin the healing process, says Golden. "Tragedy and grief metastasize and turn into the acid of hatred and legal warfare. . . . Our legal system in the traditional model teaches people to hate one another very effectively."[5]

After an environmental mishap in Massachusetts, U.S. Air Force Undersecretary of Environment Tad McCall offered the following apology: "I am sorry we polluted your water. I am sorry we have not dealt with the investigation and cleanup in the way we should have. I will take responsibility for ensuring that the Air Force makes your community whole again."[6] In three short sentences, McCall admitted the Air Force's culpability, validated the community's feelings, and began rebuilding their damaged relationship.

Likewise, N. Wayne Hale Jr., a NASA launch integration manager, delivered a heartrending expression of regret and responsibility in taking the blame for the space shuttle *Columbia* crash. In a three-page letter to NASA employees, Hale wrote, "I had the opportunity and the information and I failed to make use of it. I don't know what an inquest or a court of law would say, but I stand condemned in the court of my own conscience to be guilty of not preventing the *Columbia* disaster. We could discuss the particulars: inattention, incompetence, distraction, lack of conviction, lack of understanding, lack of backbone, laziness. The bottom line is that I failed to understand what I was being told; I failed to stand up and be counted. Therefore look no further; I am guilty of allowing *Columbia* to crash."[7]

Apologies That Don't Work

Not all who apologize are as gracious as Tad McCall or N. Wayne Hale Jr. What follows are a handful of apologies given over the years that have either made a bad situation worse or just seem to miss the point.

The Nonapology Apology.   This form of apology was used by Scott James, host of a radio program on 600 KCOL Radio, after he equated homosexuals with child molesters. "So if you're so thin-skinned that you took offense to a slip of the tongue that I had, then I offer my apology. I am sorry that you were offended."[8] James wasn't sorry for offending us, he was sorry that we're so thin-skinned.

The "It's Not Our Fault" Apology.   When asked about accidents attributed to his company's defective tires, Masatoshi Ono, CEO of Bridgestone Firestone, replied, "If we are deemed responsible for the accidents, that is another matter. However, there are maybe outside causes that had caused the accidents."[9]

The "It's Your Fault" Apology.   Former White House budget director Mitch Daniels came up with this weasel-like apology after making inflammatory comments about compensation for the family member of a 9/11 victim: "I regret if my comment was misconstrued."[10] Daniels didn't regret his comments, he regretted we were all too stupid to understand what he meant. Why even bother?

The "I Drank Too Much" Apology.   This is the apology Mel Gibson used after bad-mouthing Jews when he was stopped for reckless driving. Called to account for his anti-Semitic tirade, Mel relied on the "I have an alcohol problem" defense and pledged to confront his demons and rehabilitate his wild ways.[11] The problem is that alcohol doesn't actually make us disrespect or dislike other people, it just allows those feelings to surface.

The Groveling Apology.   In 2007, the Chinese manufacturing sector took an international beating over shoddy manufacturing practices that led to worldwide recalls of everything from tires to toothpaste. Not happy with the way its exports were portrayed in the media, Chinese officials put pressure on major manufacturers to eat crow in the international media.

Mattel, maker of Barbie dolls and other popular products, recalled more than twenty million Chinese-made toys over concerns involving lead paint and tiny magnets that toddlers could swallow. At a Beijing news conference, toy manufacturer Mattel blamed its own design flaws for the manufacturing woes in China. It was painful to watch Thomas Debrowski, Mattel's executive vice president for worldwide operations, sitting next to the Chinese official in charge of product safety, telling reporters that the problem with the toys involved Mattel's design flaws. "Mattel takes full responsibility for these recalls and apologizes personally to you, the Chinese people and all of our customers who received the toys," said Debrowski.

At the news conference, Chinese safety official Li Changjiang reveled in rubbing Mattel's nose in dirt. "I really hope that Mattel can learn lessons and gain experience from these incidents," said Changjiang, adding Mattel should "improve their control measures."[12] Mattel was willing to kowtow to the Chinese government so as not to run the risk of further alienating representatives of the world's largest market.

The "I Won't Say Why I'm Apologizing" Apology.   If you carefully read Eliot Spitzer's apology after he was caught using prostitutes, you'll see that the New York governor never once mentioned precisely what he was apologizing for:

> Good afternoon. Over the past nine years, eight years as attorney general and one as governor, I've tried to uphold a vision of progressive politics that would rebuild New York and create opportunity for all. We sought to bring real change to New York and that will continue. I want to briefly address a private matter. I have acted in a way that violates my obligations to my family and that violates my—or any—sense of right and wrong. I apologize first, and most importantly, to my family. I apologize to the public, whom I promised better. I do not believe that politics in the long run is about individuals. It is about ideas, the public good and what is best for the state of New York. But I have disappointed and failed to live up to the standard I expected of myself. I must now dedicate some time to regain the trust of my family. I will not be taking questions. Thank you very much. I will report back to you in short order. Thank you very much.[13]

Selfish or indifferent apologies like the preceding ones often do more harm than good. Instead of expressions of true regret, these apologies come across as little more than deflections of responsibility or feeble excuses for truly injurious and hurtful acts.

Biojax Part 6: An Interview Done Correctly

Knowing how easy it is to deliver the wrong message, Joan Smith, the chief executive officer of JLA Life Sciences Corporation, is about to attempt a do-over of her Chapter One interview. As a reminder, her company recently received government approval to bring Biojax, a new cancer-fighting treatment, to market. Use of the biologic is expensive, however, with each round of the treatment costing $25,000. So far, government, as well as most managed-care and insurance companies, refuse to cover the cost of Biojax. Her first attempt at addressing the controversy surrounding Biojax resulted in the following news report:

Drugmaker Denies "Gouging" Cancer Patients

"We are not greedy," claims CEO

JLA Life Sciences, maker of the recently approved drug Biojax, is insisting the high-priced oncology treatment "does not rip off" cancer patients, as critics contend. Biojax, a biologic made from living cells, is prescribed at a cost of $25,000 per treatment.

"We are not gouging cancer patients," said Joan Smith, chief executive officer for the biologic maker. Smith, who denies the company is "letting people die," blamed government for the lack of patient access to Biojax. "It's not as if Biojax is dangerous or unproven," she claimed. "Government refuses to pay for the drug because they think we priced it too high."

According to JLA's CEO, the problem is that government "is ignorant when it comes to biologic medicines." Smith blamed the drug's high cost on research and development expenses. "We are not greedy," she stated.

She does admit, however, that profit is an important factor in pricing. "A business needs to make money," she said.

Smith refused to provide specifics when asked about JLA's revenues and profits. "We're a privately owned company and I don't have to answer that." She also refused to confirm or deny that $2 million has been spent on a Biojax public relations campaign. When asked about the rumor, she snapped, "No comment."

When I first shared the news report with Joan, she was in shock. The fact is, however, that by focusing on the dramatic element in telling Joan's story the reporter did nothing wrong. Like them or not, the quotes are accurate. Fortunately for Joan, she will have an opportunity few spokespeople or newsmakers get in today's frenzied media world: a second chance at persuading stakeholders.

Both an art and a science, interviewing is a unique process. To be successful, spokespeople or newsmakers must be both responsive and proactive. They must appear accommodating, yet be unyielding. To do this, they must learn to be receptive to unfamiliar or confrontational questions while still delivering their intended messages. This requires a subtle, almost sublime ability to manage the interview and transform the interviewer into a conduit for critical ideas. Using the messages she created in Chapter Four and incorporating the techniques explained in Chapters Five and Six, Joan will attempt to strike an appropriate balance between diffusing the controversy surrounding Biojax and increasing the public's awareness of its therapeutic benefits. Following is the unedited transcript of her latest attempt at a media interview:

Interviewer: Biojax is said to be a breakthrough drug in the treatment of various forms of cancer. What is it that makes Biojax effective?

Joan Smith: Biojax is a highly effective cancer-fighting drug. Unlike traditional medicine, Biojax is a biologic, which means it's made from living cells. Eighteen hundred patients were involved in clinical studies for Biojax and the growth of cancer slowed for 60 percent of them. Biojax can help a lot of cancer patients.

Interviewer: Why is government refusing to cover the cost of Biojax?

Joan Smith: I won't speak on government's behalf and I encourage you to contact the appropriate decision makers. (*With added inflection.*) I can tell you that Biojax needs to be reimbursed so that patients can have access to an important new cancer medicine. It's sad that cancer patients are suffering because of a bureaucratic decision not to give them access to a new drug that slows the growth of cancer.

Interviewer: Is your company greedy?

Joan Smith (remembering to breathe): We wish this cancer medicine could be less expensive. (*Gestures with her hands.*) Biojax is expensive due to the high cost of manufacturing a medicine made from living cells, and government needs to help cancer patients by offering coverage for this important medicine.

Interviewer: How do you respond to critics who say that the drug's $25,000 cost rips off cancer patients?

Joan Smith (still remembering to breathe): Creating a new medicine from living cells and organisms is what makes Biojax costly. Biojax is a very effective new cancer medicine. Six out of ten patients in the clinical studies experienced a slower progression of their cancer.

Interviewer: Are you gouging cancer patients?

Joan Smith: As I said, Biojax costs what it does because of the high cost of manufacturing a new medicine made from living cells. (*Making strong eye contact.*) Again, we wish this cancer medicine cost less to produce.

Interviewer: Yet your company is being blamed for the lack of patient access to the drug because of its high cost. What's your comment?

Joan Smith (with friendly inflection): I've answered the question a couple of times and if you like, I'll answer it one last time before we move on. The cost of Biojax reflects the high cost of manufacturing a medicine from living cells. Government could help these cancer patients by ensuring those who need the drug are getting it.

Interviewer: Is your company letting people die?

Joan Smith (breathing): Excuse me?

Interviewer: I said is your company letting people die?

Joan Smith: Please help me understand the context of the question.

Interviewer: The context is straightforward. JLA Life Sciences is charging an obscene $25,000 per treatment. Cancer patients are suffering because your drug is too expensive for them to use. Care to comment?

Joan Smith: Biojax is helping some cancer patients live longer. (*Speaking slowly and pausing between ideas.*) What the drug does is slow the growth of some cancers and reduce the risk of recurrence. Through our Compassionate Care Program, we do our very best to help as many patients as we can. It's critical that patients call or write their representatives to push them to help pay for this important, new drug.

Interviewer: What were your company's revenues and profits last year?

Joan Smith: As a private company, earnings are proprietary. I can tell you that (*with emphasis*) 40 percent of patients look to government to pay for the medicines they use.

Right now, only patients of means or those with private insurance plans are able to get Biojax to treat their cancer. Cancer patients without a private drug plan are like passengers on the *Titanic*—the lifeboats are only available to passengers who can afford them.

Interviewer: Is it true that your company is spending $2 million on its PR and lobbying campaign?

Joan Smith: Specific budgets are not generally shared. I will say we are proud to dedicate significant financial resources to our overall communications programs. It's important for patients to know about all available treatment options.

Interviewer: Anything to add?

Joan Smith: Government should support cancer patients who can be helped by Biojax. Our hope is to see Biojax in the hands of those who need it.

Following the interview, I asked Joan if she felt that she was able to be responsive to the reporter's questions while still delivering her important messages. Her answer was an emphatic, "Yes." Joan believed she managed the encounter and generated positive quotes. Having read the transcript of Joan's second interview, what do you think? Did she deliver her messages? Did she convey professionalism and confidence? For a definitive answer, let's look at the resulting news report:

Drugmaker Blames Price on "High Cost of Manufacturing"

"We wish this cancer medicine could be less expensive," CEO claims

JLA Life Sciences, maker of the recently approved oncology drug Biojax, is insisting that high production expenses are to blame for the drug's $25,000 per treatment cost. "We wish this cancer medicine could be less expensive," said Joan Smith, chief executive officer for the biologic maker.

"Biojax is expensive due to the high cost of manufacturing a medicine made from living cells and government needs to help cancer patients by offering coverage for this important medicine," Smith said. "Forty percent of patients rely on government to pay for the medicines they use."

According to Smith, "Cancer patients without a private drug plan are like passengers on the *Titanic*—the lifeboats are only available to passengers who can afford them."

Of the eighteen hundred patients in the clinical trials, 60 percent experienced slower growth of their cancer. "Our hope is to see Biojax in the hands of those who need it," the CEO said.

Smith disputed claims from critics that the drug's big price tag has left cancer patients suffering. "Through our Compassionate Care Program, we do our very best to help as many patients as we can," she claimed.

Asked about JLA's revenues and profits, Smith said that "as a private company, earnings are proprietary." Regarding the rumored $2 million public relations campaign to pressure government to offer coverage for Biojax, Smith said even though "specific budgets are not generally shared," the company commits "significant financial resources" to its communications programs. "It's important for patients to know about all available treatment options," she added.

Joan's hard work and preparation have resulted in a news report that benefits both her organization and her stakeholders. Instead of depicting JLA Life Science Corporation as uncaring and greedy, the report presents the company as empathetic and ethical. By clearly conveying Joan's messages, the story not only promotes the efficacy of Biojax but also provides cancer patients and their families with the information needed to initiate positive change.

Chapter Talking Points

- When caught off-guard, breathe, listen, work to understand the problem, and then deliver a message that reflects concern. Avoid arguing or attempting to create policy on the spot.

- When confronting an industry- or sectorwide problem, use the Share the Blame Formula. The Share the Blame Formula is a structured, two-part response. The first part spreads the blame by identifying a prevalent or shared problem, then the second part takes credit for a solution.

- Use the Fluster Strategy to manage particularly difficult or antagonizing questions. The Fluster Strategy is a four-step process that provides you with more time to think while compelling the reporter to elaborate on the intent of the question. This allows you to reframe the question in a positive manner and respond with an important message.

- When the same question is repeatedly asked, use the Closure Strategy. Each step in the Closure Strategy progressively works to bring the question to a conclusion while offering you a chance to reiterate your primary message.

- Flustering questions often turn into persistent questions. When this happens use the Cluster Strategy, a combination of the Fluster Strategy and the Closure Strategy.

- When mistakes are made, it is best to own up to them with a heartfelt and genuine apology. To be heartfelt and genuine, an apology must acknowledge a failure, take responsibility, state regret, and commit to changes in behavior.

7

TWENTY WHAT-IFS

"I have been cautioned to talk but be careful not
to say anything."

—*Mark Twain*

As should be clear by now, many reporters and journalists are
skilled at duping prospective interview subjects. Leading questions, suggestive questions, and implied dilemmas are just a few
of the tricks they use to confuse spokespeople or newsmakers and
bolster a prospective story. The danger to spokespeople is when
they become increasingly frustrated with the reporter and fall
into the trap of acting defensively or ill-tempered. It can be a
classic case of winning the battle but losing the war, with trust
being a key casualty. At the same time, a potential interviewee
cannot tell a reporter, "I want to see your questions in advance,"
or "I want to see the story before you publish it." That steps over
the line and suggests a cynical desire to micromanage the story.
Therefore, spokespeople and newsmakers must be prepared to
face manipulative or misleading interviewing techniques.
Collected during sixteen years of experience as a journalist and
twenty-two years of experience as a media consultant, these
are twenty of the most frequently encountered questions and
situations that frustrate or fluster spokespeople, along with effective strategies for successfully managing them.

You Don't Know What to Say

Stammering nervously, you struggle to answer a question but fail to find the right words. It's every spokesperson's nightmare: literally tongue-tied in front of a gaggle of reporters. Sometimes it's a wayward statistic or obscure detail. Other times, it's a hit-and-run question. All spokespeople at some point will be confronted with a situation or question that leaves them at a loss for words. Following are five common situations that can stump even the most experienced spokesperson and corresponding solutions for each.

What If You Don't Want to Answer the Question, But You Have to Say Something? Bill Gates was in China to promote Microsoft, where the company initially faced an uphill battle. *Fortune Magazine* journalist David Kirkpatrick asked Gates if he was troubled by the way the Chinese government squelches free speech on the Internet and disrespects human rights. Kirkpatrick wrote, "Our conversation, which had been flowing freely, ground to a halt. He said nothing. His silence lasted so long I found myself piping up out of discomfort. 'That's a very pregnant pause,' I said." Usually it's interviewees who are unnerved by pauses and feel the need to say something. In this case, it was Kirkpatrick who felt awkward because of the silence. Gates, by the way, finally answered by saying, "I don't think I want to give an answer to that."[1] As for how he could have answered, he might have said, "I am here in China solely to focus on the creation, marketing, and distribution of software and I would be pleased to discuss that subject." Though it may not have been the answer Kirkpatrick was looking for, it was an answer in that it explained why Gates chose not to respond directly.

Though a spokesperson or newsmaker wants to be seen as honest and transparent, the interview encounter is not a confessional. When you don't want to answer a question, offer reporters a credible reason why you're unwilling to answer their question and then tell them what you would prefer to discuss. For Bill Gates, this would entail making clear that he wasn't in China to discuss political or social issues, but to sell software. Similarly, revenue from sales is not information most companies want to share. If a corporate spokesperson is asked to reveal it, an appropriate response would be, "Those numbers are proprietary. I would be happy, though, to discuss our latest marketing efforts."

What If You Don't Know How an Accident or Mistake Happened?   When bad news happens, people immediately begin pointing fingers and asking questions. Whose fault was it? Did you make a mistake? Are you negligent? The truth of the matter is that in the early stages of a problem, the answers to these questions are not yet known. Consequently, spokespeople end up saying things like "We don't know," or "Your guess is as good as mine." Those answers rarely instill confidence and greatly increase the chance that you'll be presented as the story's "village idiot." Imagine one of your sales representatives has been charged with a criminal offense and a reporter contacts you for comment. In this case, the reporter has facts that you don't. Though you lack information, you still want to avoid saying, "This is the first I'm hearing of it." Instead, when you're asked for details you don't possess, say, "Allow me an opportunity to get back to you with the latest information."

Similarly, in a situation where an injury has taken place at a manufacturing plant, reporters will want details. Because OSHA will be called in to investigate, you have an opportunity to broaden your response. Rather than answering with the equivalent of "I have no idea," it's better to say, "No one yet knows." By invoking the indefinite pronoun "no one," you avoid pointing to yourself as being uninformed while still expressing the uncertainty of the situation. Saying "No one yet knows" is truthful and makes the need to find answers bigger than you or your organization.

What If You're Asked for Hard Numbers and Don't Know the Answer?   Data, statistics, and numbers are an important component of any dialogue. Often, they're needed to support a message or persuade skeptical stakeholders. Earnings, income-expense ratios, profit-loss numbers, capital expenditures—no one can remember them all, particularly in stressful situations. But when asked about specific numbers, saying "I don't know" and stopping there won't serve you or your organization well.

When asked for numbers or statistics that you're obligated or willing to share but just don't know, respond by saying, "I want to be absolutely precise and specific, so I will need to get back to you with the exact number." Using words like "precise," "specific," and "exact" conveys that the question has been taken seriously. Just be sure to actually get back to reporters with the information they need. Otherwise, the journalist can report you failed to follow through on a pledge to provide information.

What If You Don't Know the Answer, But a Colleague Who Is with You May Know It?   Imagine you're holding a news conference with a colleague—call her Eileen. During the course of the conference you're asked, "What are the highlights of the legislation you propose?" Much to your chagrin, you're unsure of the answer. At this point, avoid immediately turning to Eileen and putting her on the spot. Why? Because now Eileen is caught off-guard. She has no time to think of what to say.

Instead, while the question is being asked, glance at Eileen to see if her expression and body language indicate that she's engaged and wants to answer the question. If Eileen's eyes signal confidence, you can respond, "I'm going to ask my colleague to address that for you." If Eileen can provide a better answer than you, but needs a moment or two to collect her briefing notes, answer, "In a moment, I am going to ask my colleague Eileen to review the highlights of the legislation for you. I can tell you that in drafting the legislation, we took a number of variables into consideration. In terms of the highlights, I'll turn it over to

Eileen." With this brief diversion, you just bought Eileen some time to collect her thoughts.

What If You Need to Pause? Most people are uncomfortable with pauses. They usually feel an obligation to keep the conversation moving so there are no socially awkward moments. The problem is that instead of pausing, people nervously jabber and say things they later wish they hadn't. If during an interview or when answering a question, you have said absolutely everything you need to say, then let there be a pause. Pausing by itself is not problematic. An interview or news conference is not a social event. The reporter is simply someone there to do a job, as are you.

How a pause is interpreted depends on the tone of the question that preceded it. For instance, if a CEO is asked about her vision for the company's future and she pauses for a few moments, the journalist could write, "The CEO paused thoughtfully when considering the company's future." However, if the question has a darker tone, such as "Are you mismanaging the company?" and is followed by a lengthy pause, the journalist could report, "The CEO paused awkwardly when asked about her mismanagement of the company." Considering the options, I go back to the old adage I wrote in my high school yearbook many years ago: "Better to remain silent and be thought a fool, than to speak up and remove all doubt."

You Shouldn't Answer at All

Day after day, journalists need to investigate leads, unravel ambiguities, and uncover new stories. It's a difficult job. In pursuit of a story, journalists ask many questions. Most are legitimate, and spokespeople and newsmakers have a responsibility to answer them in a candid, honest way. But, whether due to ethics or the law, there are some questions a spokesperson or newsmaker should not answer. This is especially true for anyone associated with professions like medicine, law, religion, psychology, and even journalism itself. This section presents a number of situations where due to circumstances or confidentiality regulations, you are better served not answering a reporter's question.

What If There Really Is Nothing to Say?   Convicted Canadian killer Karla Homolka, reviled for her part in murdering three women, including her sister, was being paroled from prison. In a jailhouse interview prior to her release, the reporter asked Homolka what she would do first upon her release. "This will sound stupid," said Homolka. "I'd like to have an iced cappuccino. An iced cappuccino from Tim Hortons—that's what I'd like to do." Well, as you can imagine, executives at the coffee and donut chain were in a tizzy, wondering whether and how they should respond to Homolka's comment. The company opted for, "We know that customers can differentiate what Tim Hortons stands for as a good community company and that there's no association between us and her."[2]

In seeking to distance itself from a convicted killer, however, the company delivered a message that clearly did not need to be delivered. When a question strikes you as absurd, irrelevant, or is clearly designed to draw you into a no-win situation, don't fall into the trap. In these types of situations, my preference for a quote is, "There's really nothing to be said." The quote avoids mentioning the company's name and makes no reference to the issue or situation in question. It also makes it clear that the situation doesn't actually deserve acknowledgment. Other response options include "I'll pass on responding" and "I have no thoughts to share on that."

What If the Answer Is Confidential?   In the world of health care, guidelines presented in the U.S. Health Information Portability and Accountability Act (HIPAA) and the Canadian Privacy Act state that health care representatives must not share details related to specific patients. If health care representatives cannot identify or talk about individual patients, how can a hospital defend itself against a specific allegation of poor patient care?

Consider a hospital facing accusations of culpability in the death of a patient who was waiting for emergency treatment. The media is under no restriction when it comes to naming the patient and interviewing aggrieved family members, but hospital officials are prohibited from commenting on the specifics of the case. To address the situation, however, a spokesperson must ensure that the hospital's perspective is reported in the media. The challenge facing the spokesperson is to get the hospital's message across while at the same time protecting the privacy of the dead patient. In this situation, a spokesperson could say, "We have the utmost respect for confidentiality rules, as well as the privacy of the family involved, so we cannot directly address this specific issue. We would just like to remind everyone that there are two sides to every story and assure people that we're doing everything we can to help the appropriate authorities resolve this issue." Though the spokesperson is unable to comment specifically on the case at hand, by explaining the confidentiality restrictions and invoking the credibility of a third party (appropriate authorities), she is still able to deliver a message that positions the hospital in a more sympathetic light.

What If It's a Question about a Rumor?   These days news is often driven by rumors, including unverified accounts of events, misinformation, smears, and calculated spin. Easily disseminated through the Internet and electronic media, rumors are spread for political purposes, business interests, financial gain, and entertainment value. These rumors often encompass everything from the irrelevant (who is dating whom) to the apocalyptic (suitcase bombs). Many rumors are harmless, but the real danger comes when a spokesperson, executive, or politician addresses one as if it was fact.

When PLO leader Yasser Arafat was languishing on his deathbed in Paris, word circulated that he had actually died, when in fact, he hadn't. Though Arafat was alive and breathing, President Bush was enticed into commenting on Arafat's death. "My first reaction is God rest his soul," said the president. Though the president's comment appears to have been genuine and heartfelt, he took as gospel something that should have been confirmed.

When asked to comment on a rumor, it's best to state that your focus is always on fact, not rumor. For example, a CEO asked to comment on reports that her company plans to acquire another company would be well-advised to respond with: "Our focus is always on facts. And in this case, the simple fact is we're continually looking to strengthen our position in the market-place and gain a competitive edge."

What If the Answer Is Personnel-Related?   Unless you work alone, odds are you or your organization will encounter personnel issues. Most will not be newsworthy, but if it involves a C-level executive, board members, or someone famous, then you should expect your personnel issue to become a news event. These types of situations can be problematic because they involve legal issues or may have market capitalization implications.

Say your CEO, Bill James, has suddenly left the company. Though senior executives will not say why Bill left, the rumor is the chief operating officer brought in to work alongside Bill has been offered a CEO position elsewhere. Not wanting to lose the COO, the board decided to give the COO the CEO job, thereby displacing Bill. Despite persistent rumors that Bill was fired, senior management has been instructed to say only that Bill James chose to move on. "Was Bill James fired?" is likely the first question a reporter will ask. In this situation, the best response is "Bill James is a talented executive and if you have questions for or about him, you might want to chat with him directly."

Commenting on someone's employment record in a negative context can often put you in legal jeopardy. Even if someone is fired with cause, detailing the circumstances of that firing to a reporter can potentially land you in court if the dismissed employee chooses to litigate. In this type of circumstance, it's almost always best to say as little as possible.

What If the Question Pertains to Lawsuits or Lost Sales? When something bad happens, it is not appropriate to talk about lawsuits, lost sales, or impacts on reputation. Consider a situation in which a reporter asks, "Are you worried about lawsuits?" After a little thought, you respond, "We aren't worried about lawsuits. Our main priority is to ensure a quick recovery for the folks involved in the accident." Sounds good. But what if the only quote used is, "We aren't worried about lawsuits"? The quote sounds dismissive and implies you have actually considered the possibility of lawsuits. Your quote about the well-being of others may never see the light of day. As discussed earlier, remember not to repeat a reporter's negatively worded question. Instead, start your response with your main message. In the above example, that message would be: "Our main priority is to ensure a quick recovery for the folks involved in the accident."

Similarly, questions about money are best left unaddressed. In these types of cases, it's better to disregard the question and try to redirect the line of questioning. For example, if a senior executive in the food industry is asked how much she expects a recall to cost her company, the most appropriate response would avoid mentioning a dollar figure and instead state, "We are prepared to take whatever steps are necessary to ensure that customers have confidence in our products."

You Have to Be Careful When Answering

Many things in life require care and concern. You need to be careful when you cross the street. You need to be careful when you install an electrical outlet. You need to be careful with your money and careful about what you eat. And by this point, it should be obvious that you always need to be careful when dealing with the media. Even with this reality clearly in mind, there are still some situations in which you need to be especially prudent. The following are not questions you should necessarily refuse to answer but instead are questions that deserve some extra consideration and care.

What If It's a Question about a Competitor?   Here's what can happen when you address questions about other people and companies. While answering a question, you thoughtfully say, "Our competitor makes a good, high-quality product. But we have an even higher level of quality in our product, coupled with greater benefits for consumers." If the reporter quotes only the first sentence, then you end up selling product for the competition. On the flip side, saying something negative about a competitor may appear petty. Instead of being drawn into a conversation about other companies, tell reporters, "I can speak only on behalf of my company and what I can tell you is . . . ," and then transition to your prepared message. Or say, "If you have questions for or about other companies, you might want to ask them. What I can tell you is . . . ," then shift the conversation to your intended message.

What If It's a General Question about a Specific Private or Privileged Situation?   Privacy laws preclude spokespeople in certain sectors from discussing specific people or situations with reporters. Banks cannot discuss individual customers, and government agencies are not at liberty to talk about a member of the public. Even though reporters know about privacy legislation, they are under no obligation to respect it. Knowing that spokespeople are sometimes limited in what they can say, journalists tell interviewees to speak generally about issues of this nature rather than focus on the specific case at hand. For example, a reporter could say, "I realize you can't discuss this particular case, but in general, how do you approach problems of this nature?" This is a slippery slope, though, because it is easy for a journalist to take comments offered in a general sense and apply them to a specific situation.

When spokespeople are asked to provide a general comment on a specific private situation, they must answer in a way that makes it difficult to be taken out of context or misinterpreted. For example, take the hypothetical case of a ten-year-old boy who died suddenly after a short fall from an amusement park ride. A neurologist interviewed about the boy's death would decline to comment on the specifics of the case, but may offer general comments on head trauma by saying, "Even a short fall could lead to a hematoma or contusion that could result in death." It is then possible for the reporter to take that comment and make it specific to the boy in question. To guard against this, the neurologist should rephrase the answer to say, "Generally speaking, even a short fall, generally speaking, could lead to a hematoma or contusion that, generally speaking, could possibly result in death." It makes for an awkward sentence, but by liberally sprinkling it with "generally speaking" you ensure the reporter does not report the comment as if you were talking about the specific case.

What If the Question Is Offensive?   Campaigning for the GOP nomination, Senator John McCain was asked a question about Hillary Clinton, who at that time was still a viable contender for the Democratic nomination. "How do we beat the bitch?" asked an audience member. "That's an excellent question," responded McCain. Excuse me? What is so "excellent" about calling a female presidential candidate a bitch? By answering as he did, McCain confirmed he was like-minded with the questioner in believing that Clinton was indeed a bitch. Considering the question and answer were heard in a public forum, at the very least McCain was obligated to respond to the characterization about Clinton. More appropriate comments or responses would have been:

- "Hillary Clinton deserves to be treated with dignity and respect."
- "Your terminology is inappropriate."
- "Hillary Clinton is a respected member of the Senate."

This does not mean that any time an offensive question is asked, you must pick up the mantle and fight back. In some instances, it can be a trap. For example, if reporters are conducting an interview for print or recording an interview for TV or radio, their questions are likely to be edited out. With that in mind, reconsider the earlier question: "How do you plan to beat that bitch, Hillary Clinton?" Rightfully offended, you answer, "I never said Hillary Clinton is a bitch." Then, after setting the questioner straight, you offer an in-depth explanation of your strategy for victory. You don't need a journalism degree from Columbia University to figure out which quote the reporter will use: "I never said Hillary Clinton is a bitch." Even though the respondent believes he is doing something positive by refuting the offensive claim, he makes it worse for himself by accepting the premise of the question.

Better to respond with one of the three choices offered above, as Senator McCain himself discovered when a similar situation repeated itself. At a Cincinnati rally, conservative radio host Bill Cunningham was invited to introduce the senator as a guest speaker. In his introductory remarks, Cunningham made disparaging comments about then-candidate Barack Obama, and in an obvious attempt to remind people of Obama's Muslim roots, made repeated references to Obama's middle name, which is Hussein. Still licking his wounds from the Hillary Clinton incident, Senator McCain condemned Cunningham's remarks and expressed his respect for both Senator Obama and Senator

Clinton. Fool me once, shame on you. Fool me twice, shame on me.

What If You Are Asked for Your Personal Opinion? Unless your opinion directly matches the policy of the organization you represent, it is best not to offer one. Major General Peter Pace, Chairman of the U.S. Joint Chiefs of Staff, learned that the hard way after calling homosexuality immoral while defending the military's "Don't ask, don't tell" policy. "I should have focused more on my support of the policy and less on my personal moral views," General Pace later said.[3] As a result of his comment, General Pace faced a flurry of condemnation from many senior politicians and civil libertarians. Defense Secretary Robert Gates did a much better job of handling the question when he was asked his view of the policy: "I think personal opinion really doesn't have a place here."[4]

What If the Issue Is Ugly, But You're Not the Appropriate Spokesperson?   In a global environment where every large corporation sources products from developing nations or has investments in other countries, it is possible to have a controversial situation occur outside the sphere of your own organization and still be associated with it. Those situations may include everything from an environmental disaster caused by the actions of a global subsidiary to sexually explicit comments made by a fellow politician.

For example, Justin works for a global company that has invested more than $2 billion in Australia to build factories on land that until recently belonged to aboriginals. Critics accuse the Australian government of relocating thousands of aboriginal tribe members who had occupied the land for generations to make way for industry. Critics say the company is responsible for the forced removal of indigenous people. Justin, who is vice president of government affairs, does not want the Australian story to become an issue in the United States. In an interview,

Justin is asked, "Is your company responsible for the forced removal of indigenous people?" In this instance, Justin's best option is to simply answer, "We respect the rights of aboriginal people worldwide. For information about Australia, your best bet is to contact our head office there." Though Justin does not directly address the Australian situation, his response positions the company in a favorable light.

What If You Don't Like What You're Saying?   Never feel obligated to complete a sentence. Whether caused by a lost thought or an incidental distraction, a partial sentence need not be finished. Simply stop and begin the response again. A reporter is unlikely to quote a half-delivered sentence as opposed to a full sentence, unless the answer you were giving was substantially different from your second response. For instance, if during an interview you start to say, "I didn't realize that what I was doing was against—" and you stop. Then, you continue with, "I have always obeyed the law." It's clear that the two answers do not match. The first sentence appears to claim ignorance, while the second one flatly denies any wrongdoing. Since the second answer contradicts what the first sentence was starting to say, the journalist would be justified in reporting your half sentence.

If you complete a comment and then realize your answer was inappropriate or did not come out as planned, you have the option of telling the reporter: "Let me try that again. I know I can be even clearer." Then correct yourself by delivering the answer you intended. But do not expect a guarantee that the reporter will ignore the first comment, especially if it fits the intended story.

It's a Trick Question

Trick questions are questions meant to purposely entrap, confuse, or mislead the interviewee. More specifically, a trick question presupposes or implies something negative, then presents this implication as a question that limits possible replies to those that serve the reporter's agenda. "Do you still beat your wife?" is a classic example of a trick question. It rightly or wrongly implies that you have beaten your wife, and whether you answer it in the positive ("Yes, I still beat my wife") or the negative ("No, I don't still beat my wife"), you unavoidably confirm the implication or fallacy. Reporters have many ways of entrapping spokespeople, but here are three of the most common and possibly damaging.

What If It's a "Yes or No" Question? Reporters like asking yes-no questions. Also known as polar questions, yes-no questions are intended to be answered definitively yes or no. Yes-no questions get right to the point. If people are honest, they should have no reason not to answer yes-no questions, right? While yes-no questions are necessary in the court of law, in the court of public opinion they do not always get to the truth of an issue. Trying to pin down interviewees by having them proffer yes-no answers turns issues into black and white when sometimes situations are more a shade of grey.

Let's first look at the word "no." Consider the question, "Yes or no, does your drug have deadly side effects?" The most likely answer is "No, our drug is safe." But based on the answer, the quote could read, "'No,' snapped Ansell when asked whether his drug has deadly side effects." Once again, answering with the word "no" has a spokesperson accepting the premise of an offensive question and lends credence to the integrity of the question.

While the word "no" is problematic, the word "yes" has even greater negative impact. For example, a reporter could ask, "Yes or no, can use of your new medication result in harmful side effects?" An honest answer to this question would be, "Yes, but the chances of that are minimal to nonexistent." Based on that response, the resulting media quote could read, "'Yes,' says drugmaker when asked if the drug has harmful side effects." What about the part of the answer that says the risk of side effects is minimal to nonexistent? Not surprisingly, that part of the quote failed to survive the media edit.

In another example, a client of mine in the energy sector was accused, but never convicted, of engaging in misleading sales tactics. Recognizing a problem, the company altered sales practices to ensure greater integrity. Years after the problem was addressed, however, reporters continued to bring up the negative history regarding sales. Because the problem had been resolved years earlier, there was no real need to talk about the issue. Talking about it would have only prolonged the wrongs of the past. But on occasion, reporters would still ask, "Yes or no, was your company convicted for using deceptive sales practices?" An appropriate response was to simply say, "That wasn't the case." This answer is not as defensive-sounding and is much less quotable than "no."

What If It's an "Is It Possible" Question?   The phrase "is it possible" is a classic setup for a verbal sucker punch. Imagine a journalist asks a nuclear engineer, "Is it possible a Chernobyl-type radiation release could happen at the local nuclear power plant?" Engineers, who tend to take questions very literally, will invariably respond, "Yes, it is possible." That quote however, conveys an impression of imminent danger where none exists and will trigger concern, if not panic, on the part of stakeholders.

Or, imagine your company stores confidential computer information with customers' bank account details, social security numbers, and other private data. At a news conference, a reporter asks, "Is it possible a hacker could break into your computer and steal confidential customer information?" After careful consideration, you answer, "It is possible. You should know, however, that the security measures we have in place make a breach of privacy highly unlikely." Well, you just know the headline is going to focus on the "it is possible" part of the answer and is likely to read, "Spokesperson confirms, breach of privacy is possible." True, the "it is possible" part of the response is honest, but your message about existing security measures is conveniently missing. No matter how a spokesperson responds to an "is it possible" question, the comment is newsworthy. A "yes" answer exposes the quote to the uncertainties of the media edit, while a "no" answer just doesn't sound credible: "No, it is not possible security could be breached." This answer sounds blatantly dishonest and deceitful.

How to answer instead? First, present your message. In this case, "The security measures we have in place are designed to preserve and protect privacy." If that doesn't satisfy the reporter, which it probably won't, then use the Closure Strategy as presented in Chapter Six:

Reporter: Is it possible a hacker could break into your computer system and steal confidential customer information?

Spokesperson: The security measures we have in place are designed to preserve and protect privacy.

Reporter: Yes, but is it possible a hacker could break into your computer system and steal confidential customer information?

Spokesperson: As I said, our security measures ensure a high degree of privacy.

Reporter: You're not answering my question. Is it possible a hacker could break into your computer system and steal confidential customer information?

Spokesperson: I've answered the question a couple of times and if you like, I'll answer it one last time before we move on. Security is very important to us and the safeguards we use ensure the highest degree of protection possible.

The responses offered here do in fact answer the question, only they are not the responses the reporter hoped would be given. The reporter wanted the spokesperson to either say "it is possible" or "it isn't possible." If the price of convincing the reporter that you have answered his question is to sheepishly admit "it is possible," then the price is too high.

"Yes-No" and "Is It Possible" Exception to the Rule

This is not to suggest that newsmakers should never answer "yes-no" or "is it possible" questions. "Yes-no" and "is it possible" answers should be provided when a newsmaker or company is mired in an issue or controversy where:

- The level of concern is very high.
- The level of trust is very low.
- The newsmaker's or company's ability to carry on its day-to-day affairs is severely impaired.
- The news story is on Page 1 above the fold.
- Lawmakers are discussing the issue in Congress or the legislature.

What If It's a "Can You Guarantee" Question?   Another three words to be on guard for are "can you guarantee." A "can you guarantee" question is frequently a setup because despite the question, chances are you cannot make guarantees about it. Spokespeople try to dodge "can you guarantee" questions by responding with every synonym in the thesaurus for guarantee. They will say, "I can assure you" or "I can pledge to you." Avoiding use of the word "guarantee" is by itself suspect. So what to do?

The head of a pharmaceutical company manufacturing a much-needed flu vaccine is asked whether she can guarantee that no one will die from allergic reactions to the vaccine. Possible responses include the following:

- "Yes, I can guarantee no deaths." (which she can't)
- "No, I can't guarantee there won't be deaths." (which will alarm people)
- "No one can make that guarantee." (which almost sounds like an excuse)

Each answer fails to convey the message that the vaccine saves lives and safeguards communities. Presuming the vaccine has experienced no problems in the recent past, then there is no newsworthy context for the "guarantee" question to be asked. A more appropriate answer, given the context, would be, "What I can guarantee is that our products save lives and give families much-needed peace of mind." Repeating the word "guarantee" renders the answer more responsive to the question. Conversely, not repeating the word rings alarm bells and indicates a sense of evasiveness.

Obviously, the trick is to deflect the question away from a situation that cannot possibly be guaranteed and redirect it to a guarantee that reflects your intended message. Can you guarantee a hacker won't break into your computer system and steal confidential customer information? Not credibly. Every computer system has the potential to be hacked. In this case, an effective response would be, "What I can *guarantee* is that security is very important to us and the safeguards we use ensure the highest degree of protection possible."

An important variation of the preceding strategy occurs when there is a legitimate context for the "can you guarantee" question to be asked. In the event that there have been some serious allergic reactions to your vaccine, answering the "can you guarantee" question now has newsworthy relevance. If asked whether any deaths could result, the appropriate response would be, "The guarantee we're making is that we do everything in our power to ensure that our products are safe and effective. We are working with health authorities to determine what specifically

happened in these cases." This answer accomplishes three important objectives. It directly answers the "guarantee" question
without admitting "I can't guarantee that," or defensively saying,
"No one can guarantee that." It demonstrates the taking of
action to ensure safe products. And finally, it highlights the need
to find answers by working with authorities, who at the moment
have greater credibility.

Quotus Interruptus

Interruptions happen. Some are accidental or unintentional, like
a technical glitch or an unexpected phone call. But some interruptions are an intentional, manipulative tactic to frustrate or
fluster a newsmaker.

What If You're Interrupted Mid-Answer?   What if in the
middle of giving a good answer, the journalist interrupts you, not
allowing you to finish your answer or deliver your message? The
first time you're interrupted, let it go. The second time you're
interrupted, say, "Excuse me, please allow me to complete my
thought." Then start delivering the message again from the
beginning of the sentence. That way the message is delivered in
its entirety.

If the interviewer continues to interrupt you, try gently
touching his arm. People generally freeze in their tracks when
someone unexpectedly touches them. It's an amazingly effective
technique. Try it in a relaxed social situation some time and
you'll see how helpful it can be. If after that the reporter persists
in interrupting your flow, then say, "You asked me a question—
allow me the courtesy of a response." All this presumes, of course,
that you are being responsive to the questions being asked and
are also being interesting. If you are not, the journalist has every
right to interrupt you.

Exhibit 7.1 lists a convenient summary of all twenty questions and their corresponding response strategies.

Exhibit 7.1. Twenty What-Ifs Strategy Summary

1. **What if you don't want to answer the question, but you have to say something?** Offer a credible reason why you are unwilling to answer the question and identify what you prefer to discuss.

2. **What if you don't know how an accident or mistake happened?** Answer by saying, "No one yet knows." By invoking the indefinite pronoun "no one," you avoid pointing to yourself as being uninformed.

3. **What if you're asked for hard numbers and don't know the answer?** Explain, "I want to be absolutely precise and specific, so I will need to get back to you with the exact number." Words like "precise," "specific," and "exact" convey that the question has been taken seriously.

4. **What if you don't know the answer, but a colleague who is with you may know it?** Look to see if that colleague is engaged and wants to answer the question. If so, pass the question. If he or she needs a moment, briefly discuss a related subject, then pass the question.

5. **What if you need to pause?** If you have said absolutely everything you need to say, then let there be a pause.

6. **What if there really is nothing to say?** If a question strikes you as absurd, irrelevant, or is clearly designed to draw you into a no-win situation, simply tell the reporter, "There's really nothing to be said."

7. **What if the answer is confidential?** Explain that confidentiality rules must be respected, so you cannot directly address the issue at hand. If it's relevant to the situation, consider adding, "We would just like to assure people that we're doing everything we can to help the appropriate authorities resolve this issue."

8. **What if it's a question about a rumor?** When asked to comment on a rumor, it is best to not respond at all. Instead, state that your focus is always on fact, not rumor.

9. **What if the answer is personnel-related?** It's generally best to say as little as possible because commenting on someone's

employment record in a negative context can potentially put you in legal jeopardy.

10. **What if the question pertains to lawsuits or lost sales?** Remember not to repeat words like "lawsuits" or "sales" and instead reiterate that "our main priority is to ensure the well-being of those affected" by the situation.

11. **What if it's a question about a competitor?** Inform reporters you can only speak for your company or organization and then transition to your prepared messages.

12. **What if it's a general question about a specific private or privileged situation?** Liberally sprinkle your answer with "generally speaking" to ensure the reporter does not report the comment as if you were talking about the specific case.

13. **What if the question is offensive?** Avoid directly repeating or refuting the offensive claim. If you repeat or refute it, you accept the premise of the question. Instead, express respect for the person or group insulted by the question, presuming they're worthy of it.

14. **What if you are asked for your personal opinion?** Unless your opinion directly matches the policy of the organization you represent, it is best not to offer one.

15. **What if the issue is ugly, but you're not the appropriate spokesperson?** Do not directly address the situation. Instead, offer a response that positions your company in a favorable light.

16. **What if you don't like what you're saying?** Never feel obligated to complete a sentence or thought. Simply begin the response again.

17. **What if it's a "yes or no" question?** Starting a response with the words "yes" or "no" could be a problem if reporters choose to quote only those words and edit out what follows. Unless the question relates to a high-concern or low-trust issue, skip "yes" or "no" and go right to the message that would follow.

18. **What if it's an "is it possible" question?** First, present your message. If that doesn't satisfy the reporter, then use the Closure Strategy as presented in Chapter Six.

19. **What if it's a "can you guarantee" question?** Avert the question from a situation that cannot possibly be guaranteed and redirect it to a "guarantee" that reflects your intended message.
20. **What if you're interrupted mid-answer?** The first time, let it go. The second time, ask to be allowed to finish your thought. If it continues, gently touch the reporter's arm. If the reporter still persists, politely demand to be given the courtesy of a response.

Sign Off

Recently on a flight from Toronto to Los Angeles, I struck up a conversation with my seatmate, actor Eddie Griffin, who has starred in the movies *Deuce Bigalow* and *Undercover Brother*. Griffin had been in the news for crashing a $1.5 million Ferrari during a practice lap at a California speedway. Walking away from the car unscathed, the comedian jokingly told reporters, "Undercover Brother's good at karate and all the rest of that, but the brother can't drive." Hearing that I was writing a book on media communication, Griffin offered this thought: "Angelina Jolie and Brad Pitt going on another trip to pick up a child is not news. Donald Trump buying a new house is not news. This is the dumbing down of the United States of America done by a news media" that is "all about WMDs, weapons of mass distraction."

Though funny, Griffin's statement is startlingly accurate. Unbiased reporting has given way to sensationalism, titillation, and partisanship. Context and meaning have become a casualty of a reporting style that transforms complex individuals into simple archetypes and turns shades of grey into black and white. Compromise is "defeat." Those who differ from us ideologically are "evil." And every disagreement is a zero sum game with clear "winners" and "losers." Add an angry and outraged public to the mix, and the communications cocktail that results can be volatile. Imperfect as news reporting is, however, President Thomas Jefferson had it right when he said he would rather have newspapers without government than government without newspapers.[5] In a free society, people should have the opportunity to express their viewpoints and be held accountable for their words or actions.

When companies are able to demonstrate to stakeholders that they hold themselves to high standards of integrity, they are better able to connect with reporters to promote their values and, in turn, sell product. There is a price to pay for engaging the media, though. When times aren't so good, companies must still interact with reporters, only it's not necessarily to sell product as much as it is to sell their credibility. In other words, the price for positive news coverage is that spokespeople must be available for negative news coverage. This means CEOs, politicians, and PR professionals must be ready to answer tough questions, provide information, or quell false rumors at a moment's notice.

When bad news happens, can a company or spokesperson ultimately win a war with the media? Don't even try—reporters buy ink by the barrel. But a larger number of companies and sectors could perhaps score the occasional "win" if they redefine what winning looks like. If at the end of the day, critics feel that a spokesperson or an organization acknowledged their concerns, demonstrated a genuine desire to find common ground, and acted with decency, then that is a victory. These types of real victories can be achieved through stories of newsmakers and spokespeople who "do the right thing" during a crisis. So when the headline is you, use what you've learned in this book. Get on the front page, take your hit (you probably deserved it anyway), and with any luck, tomorrow it will be lining the bottom of a birdcage.

Appendix: Media Messaging Toolkit

The Media Messaging Toolkit provides all the guidance, suggested language, and reproducible templates needed to craft a comprehensive range of effective media messages. The kit starts with the Value Compass, an abridged set of Value Compass instructions, and a list of Value Compass words. Introduced in Chapter Two, the Value Compass is a guide to identifying the values and ideals your organization hopes to project to the public.

Next is the Problem Solution Formula template, a simple framework for creating your own Problem Solution Formula message. Presented in Chapter Three, the Problem Solution Formula is a structured response that allows you to honestly address a problem while still ensuring that the solution will be quoted.

Following the Problem Solution Formula template is the Compelling Message Creator, a tool for crafting a broad selection of quotable messages that assure you the opportunity to present your organization's agenda in a proactive manner. For definitions and examples of each type of message, refer to Chapter Four.

Each of these tools can be used separately if needed, but they are designed to work together to ensure that your messages align with your organization's values and agenda. For a more in-depth look at each tool, as well as illustrative examples that facilitate implementation, refer to the tool's corresponding chapter.

The Value Compass

Value
Compass

_____
_____
_____

_____

Stakeholder(s)

N NATURE

WELL-BEING **W** STAKE SPOKESPERSON HOLDERS **E** EMOTIONS

_____
_____
_____

_____
_____
_____

STANDARDS **S**

_____
_____
_____

_____ _____ _____ _____

N **E** **W** **S**

Spokesperson's
Nature

Stakeholder's
Emotion

Stakeholder's
Well-being

Spokesperson's
Standards

© Jeff Ansell 2010

Value Compass Instructions

Step 1: Start by filling in the blank "Stakeholder(s)" line. Your stakeholders are the people most affected by your news or the people you hope to address with your message.

Step 2: Next, begin filling in the north-south axis. This is the "Spokesperson" axis that comprises (N)ature and (S)tandards. Start with (N)ature. By nature, I mean the characteristics, including ways of thinking and feeling, you want to present to the public.

Step 3: Once you decide on three words to describe your nature, move to the blank lines for (S)tandards. Broadly speaking, standards refer to a set of requirements, ideals, or a model of excellence. More specifically, standards should be exceptional principles and practices you wish to project to the public.

Step 4: Next, move to the "stakeholders" axis. Start by identifying your stakeholders' (E)motions. To do this, try imagining the feelings and reactions created by your issue or news event.

Step 5: After identifying your stakeholders' emotions, determine what it will take to enhance or ensure their (W)ell-being. What can you and your organization do or say to address their emotions, concerns, and needs?

Step 6: Once you have filled in three words for each direction, work through the categories again and choose one term from each that best reflects your desired image and your stakeholders' perspective. This process should be done in a slightly different order than filling in the initial categories. For this step, start with (N)ature, then do (E)motion, next do (W)ell-being, and finish with (S)tandards. These four words now constitute a "NEWS" filter to use as you create media messages and prepare to address the public.

Value Compass Words

Nature	*Emotions*	*Well-being*	*Standards*
Authentic	Affection	Acceptance	Accountable
Benevolent	Anger	Action	Articulate
Caring	Contempt	Comfort	Capable
Charitable	Disappointment	Commitment	Competent
Compassionate	Discouraged	Confidence	Conscientious
Concerned	Disgust	Contentment	Courteous
Considerate	Distrust	Education	Credible
Empathetic	Embarrassment	Growth	Diligent
Forthcoming	Envy	Health	Ethical
Generous	Fear	Help	Informed
Genuine	Frustration	Hope	Knowledgeable
Honest	Optimism	Information	Principled
Humble	Pride	Involvement	Professional
Intelligent	Relief	Performance	Reliable
Kind	Remorse	Production	Respectful
Open	Sadness	Profit	Responsible
Sincere	Shame	Protection	Responsive
Straightforward	Shock	Responsiveness	Scrupulous
Tolerant	Surprise	Safety	Trustworthy
Understanding	Worry	Security	Truthful

The Problem Solution Formula

The Problem Solution Formula Template

The Problem Solution Formula is a structured response that joins the problem and solution in one sentence. It is generally made up of two clauses or phrases joined by conjunctions such as "and," "so," and "though." The first clause identifies and frames the problem while the second clause offers a solution to the problem. To optimize the Problem Solution Formula, the message should be filtered through your Value Compass.

Value Compass stakeholders: _____

Value Compass terms:

| _____ | _____ | _____ | _____ |
| N | E | W | S |

To ensure your Problem Solution Formula message stays on the course charted by your Value Compass, match it to the appropriate four principles for building trust.
- Show humility.
- Answer honestly.
- Acknowledge skepticism.
- Couple concern with commitment to action.

Problem: _____

_____

Solution: _____

_____

Problem Solution Formula message: _____

_____

_____

_____

Reminders:

- Does your Problem Solution Formula message reflect your Value Compass words and speak to your stakeholders?
- Does your Problem Solution Formula message align with the four principles for building trust?
- Will your Problem Solution Formula message survive the media edit?

The Compelling Message Creator

The Compelling Message Creator Template

The News Is . . . _____

_____

Value Compass Words (Chapter Two):

_____   _____   _____   _____

N   E   W   S

Problem Solution Formula message (Chapter Three): "_____

_____ "

Your News Is . . . "_____

_____ "

Tell Your Story in Three Short Sentences:

1. "_____ "
2. "_____ "
3. "_____ "

What the News Means to Stakeholders Message: "_____

_____ "

Three Fact Messages:

1. "_____ "
2. "_____ "
3. "_____ "

Context Color Message: "_____

_____ "

Concern Color Message: "_____

_____ "

Absolute Color Message: "_____
_____"

Figurative Color Message: "_____
_____"

Call to Action Message: "_____
_____"

"If Asked . . ." Message:
If asked: "_____
_____?"

Answer: "_____
_____"

Notes

Introduction

1. Buffet, W. "Quotations on Trust." http://www.trustispower
.com/quotes/quotes.htm#biz_ldrs. 2009.

Chapter 1: What Is News?

1. Broder, D. S. *Behind the Front Page: A Candid Look at How News Is Made*. New York: Simon & Schuster, 1981.
2. Don Henley. *I Can't Stand Still*. Warner Chappell, 1982. LP.
3. Raspberry, W. "Minnesota News Council Newsletter." Fall 1994, p. 5.
4. Baldwin, K. "Blair Attacks 'Feral' Media He Once Tamed." http://uk.reuters.com/article/idUKL1285070620070612. June 2000.
5. "PR Week/PR Newswire Media Survey." *PR Week Magazine*, Apr. 6, 2009, pp. 14–15.
6. Schonfeld, E. "Six Months In, and 600 Posts Later . . . The Worlds of Blogging and Journalism Collide (in My Brain)." http://www.techcrunch.com/2008/03/30/six-months-in-and
-600-posts-later-the-worlds-of-blogging-and-journalism
-collide-in-my-brain/. Mar. 2008.
7. Cox, A. M. "Matt Drudge." *Time Magazine*, May 8, 2006, p. 97.
8. Johnson, P. "Bloggers to Join Mainstream at the Conventions." http://www.usatoday.com/life/columnist/
mediamix/2004-07-13-media-mix_x.htm. July 2004.

9. *Bill Moyers Journal*. New York: WNET, Feb. 6, 2009.

10. Stackhouse, J. "Editorial." *Globe and Mail*, May 26, 2009, p. A3.

11. Mitroff, I. *Why Some Companies Emerge Stronger and Better from a Crisis*. San Francisco: AMACOM, 2005.

12. Davies, P., Lublin, J., Martinez, B., Wilke, J., Gray, S., Winstein, K., and Sender, H. *Wall Street Journal*, June 16, 2005, pp. 1, A1, A3, B1, B7, and C1.

13. Weber Shandwick. "Risky Business: Reputations Online." http://www.online-reputations.com/DLS/RiskyBusiness _WhitePaper_US.pdf. 2009.

14. Gaines-Ross, L. "Safeguarding Reputation." http://www .webershandwick.com/resources/ws/misc/safe_rep_pp06 .pdf. Issue No 3, 2007.

15. O'Brien, K. "Edelman Trust Barometer." http://www .prweekus.com/edelman-trust-barometer-finds-ngos-are -the-most-trusted-organizations/article/51488/. Jan. 2005.

16. "PR Week/Burson-Marsteller CEO Survey 2004." Burson-Marsteller, Nov. 8, 2004.

17. Martin, D. "Open Season on Ottawa's Flacks." *National Post*, Feb. 1, 2008.

18. Fitza, M. "Sarbanes-Oxley Requirement for Outside Directors May Help Boost Pay of Celebrity CEOs." Paper presented at Leeds School of Business, Boulder, Colorado, Nov. 2007.

Chapter 2: You Are the Story

1. Fraser, J. "Beware, The Media Are Not Your Pals." *National Post*, Dec. 23, 1999.

2. Hallerman, D. "U.S. Advertising Spending." http://www .emarketer.com/Reports/All/Emarketer_2000615.aspx. Dec. 2009.

3. "White Paper: A Primer in Social Media." http://www .smashlab.com/papers/item/p/list6ItemID/v/3. Mar. 2008.

4. Tiku, N. "When Scandal Strikes." *Inc. Magazine*, Aug. 2007, p. 26.
5. "Yanking DQ Spot Falls Short." http://www.canada.com/ story_print.html?id=bac25c1d-b517-42ff-815d -9a539d80c422&sponsor. Apr. 2007.
6. Rice, R. "Tim Hortons Officials Sorry for Ad Blunder." *Bangor Daily News*, Sept. 16, 2005, p. 1.
7. Arnst, C. "On the Hot Seat at Biogen." http://www .businessweek.com/magazine/content/05_12/b3925109 .htm. Mar. 2005.

Chapter 3: How to Admit Bad News

1. Golden, J., Moy, H. A., and Lyons, A. "The Negotiation Counsel Model: An Empathetic Model for Settling Catastrophic Personal Injury Cases." *Harvard Negotiation Law Review*, 2001, 4(1–2), 236.
2. Ferrin, D. L., Kim, P. H., Cooper, C. D., and Dirks, K. T. "Silence Speaks Volumes: The Effectiveness of Reticence in Comparison to Apology and Denial for Responding to Integrity and Competence-Based Trust Violations." *Journal of Applied Psychology*, 2007, 92(4), 893–908.
3. Orth, M. "Black Mischief." http://www.vanityfair.com/ politics/features/2007/02/black200702. Feb. 2007.
4. Tedesco, T. "Black's Sharp Tongue Silences: More He Speaks, More Likely His Co-Accused Will Not." http:// www.financialpost.com/scripts/story.html?id=48613be3 -faa8-4f0e-92a0-1a1d71c45b20&k=37963&p=1. May 2007.
5. Stern, A. "Ex-Hollinger Director Urged Conrad Black Be 'Humble.'" http://www.reuters.com/article/idUSN2623462 820070428. Apr. 2007.
6. Waldie, P. "A Picture of the Beneficent Lord Black." http://v1.theglobeandmail.com/servlet/story/RTGAM .20071129.wblack29/BNStory/International/home. Nov. 2007.

7. "Wal-Mart Loses Discount Edge in Sluggish Holiday Sales." *African Connection Newspaper*, Dec. 1–15, 2004, p. 10.
8. McNatt, R. "Chrysler: Not Quite So Equal." *BusinessWeek Magazine*, Nov. 13, 2000, p. 14.
9. Kearns Goodwin, D. *Team of Rivals: The Political Genius of Abraham Lincoln.* New York: Simon & Schuster, 2005.
10. Henry, M. "Dorm Rapes Stun York U." http://www.thestar .com/printarticle/254607. Sept. 2007.
11. McArthur, K. "Canadian Brewer Molson Inc's Proposed Merger May Lack Sufficient Support." http://findarticles .com/p/articles/mi_m0EUY/is_34_10/ai_n12449528/?tag =content;coll. Sept. 2004.
12. McGinn, D. "Father Fixit." http://www.newsweek.com/ id/64499/page/1. May 13, 2002.

Chapter 4: Crafting Compelling Messages

1. Weaver, K., Garcia, S., Schwarz, N., and Miller, D., "Inferring the Popularity of an Opinion from Its Familiarity: A Repetitive Voice Can Sound Like a Chorus." *Journal of Personality and Social Psychology*, 2007, 92(5), 821–833.
2. "Come Again?" http://news.bbc.co.uk/2/hi/7138145.stm. Dec. 2007.
3. Solis, B. "Communications 2.0—Apple and the iPhone Bomb," http://www.briansolis.com/2007/09/crisis -communications-20-apple-and/. Sept. 2007.
4. "13 Most Dreadful Buzzwords." http://www.buzzwhack.com/ inside/mostdreadful.htm. Dec. 2006.
5. "Gas Prices and Fuel Economy Facts." http://retail .petro-canada.ca/en/independent/2065.aspx.
6. Kirby, J., and Engelhart, K. "Rupert Murdoch Versus the Internet." *Macleans Magazine*, Jan. 18, 2010, p. 28.
7. Sigmund, J. "Newspaper Web Sites Attract 74 Million Visitors in Third Quarter." http://www.naa.org/PressCenter/

SearchPressReleases/2009/NEWSPAPER-WEB-SITES
-ATTRACT-74-MILLION-VISITORS-IN-THIRD
-QUARTER.aspx.Oct. 2009.

8. Matthews, O. "Just an Understudy?" http://www.newsweek
.com/id/112769. Feb. 2008.

9. Taub, S. "Andersen Employees Blame Duncan." http://www
.cfo.com/article.cfm/3003126. Jan. 2002.

10. Byers, J. "Summit 'Clear Wake Up Call.'" http://www
.thestar.com/News/article/215292. May 2007.

11. Seelye, K. Q. "Barack Obama Admits He Inhaled." http://
www.nytimes.com/2006/10/24/world/americas/24iht
-dems.3272493.html. Oct. 24, 2006.

Chapter 5: Delivering Your Message

1. Ferguson, R. "I'm Sorry, Smitherman Says." http://www
.thestar.com/News/Ontario/article/307727. Feb. 2005.

2. Taber, J. "Turtle Talk Wins the Race." http://www
.theglobeandmail.com/life/article669604.ece. Feb. 2008.

3. Mehrabian, A., and Wiener, M. "Decoding of Inconsistent
Communications." *Journal of Personality and Social Psychology*,
1967, 6(1), 109–114.

4. Begley, S. "When It's Head Versus Heart, The Heart Wins."
Newsweek, Feb. 11, 2008.

5. Linkon, N. "Public Relations Basics: Developing Key
Messages for Media Interviews." http://www.ereleases.com/
prfuel/public-relations-basics-developing-key-messages-for
-media-interviews/. Dec. 2008.

6. Kurtz, H. "What's the Frequency?" http://www
.bizwashington.com/wp-dyn/articles/A37827-2004Sep21
.html. Sept. 2004.

7. Hampton, L. "I Am Not a Crook." http://www.speaktolead
.com. 2006.

8. Weaver, K., Garcia, S., Schwarz, N., and Miller, D.,
"Inferring the Popularity of an Opinion from Its Familiarity:

A Repetitive Voice Can Sound Like a Chorus." *Journal of Personality and Social Psychology*, 2007, 92(5), 821–833.

9. "Extending an Apology." *Harper's Magazine*, Sept. 2001, pp. 29–30.

Chapter 6: When the Going Gets Tough

1. "CBC Marketplace." Toronto, Canada: Canadian Broadcasting Company, Oct. 6, 1998.
2. "Extending an Apology." *Harper's Magazine*, Sept. 2001, pp. 29–30.
3. "Apology Act Would Reduce Lawsuits: MPP." http://www .thestar.com/News/Canada/article/414992. Apr. 2008.
4. "The Sorry Laws." http://www.inc.com/magazine/20060601/ handson-managing-sidebar.html. June 2006.
5. Golden, J., Moy, H. A., and Lyons, A. "The Negotiation Counsel Model: An Empathetic Model for Settling Catastrophic Personal Injury Cases." *Harvard Negotiation Law Review*, 2001, 4(1–2), 236.
6. Field, P., Moore, L., and Daw, R. "Apology a Tool for Conflict Resolution?" http://www.epa.gov/ciconference/ 2009/download/presentations/ApologyJuly09.pdf. July 2009.
7. Ibid.
8. Alford, H. "Regrets Only." http://www.nytimes.com/ 2007/10/14/opinion/14alford.html. Oct. 2007.
9. Ackman, D. "Bridgestone's Ono Out of the Fire." http:// www.forbes.com/2000/10/10/1010topnews.html. Oct. 2000.
10. Hernandez, R. "A Renewed Pledge of Aid, and a Mea Culpa." http://www.nytimes.com/2002/02/06/nyregion/ a-renewed-pledge-of-aid-and-a-mea-culpa.html? pagewanted=1. Feb. 2002.
11. "Gibson: 'I Am Not an Anti-Semite.'" http://www.cnn .com/2006/SHOWBIZ/Movies/07/31/gibson.dui/index .html. Aug. 2006.

12. Gee, M. "From Mattel, an Apology Made in China." *Globe and Mail*, Sept. 22, 2007, p. B8.

13. Chan, S. "I Apologize to the Public." http://cityroom.blogs.nytimes.com/2008/03/10/i-apologize-to-the-public/. Mar. 2008.

Chapter 7: Twenty What-Ifs

1. Kirkpatrick, D. "How Microsoft Conquered China." http://money.cnn.com/magazines/fortune/fortune_archive/2007/07/23/100134488/index2.htm. July 2007.

2. Brent, P. "Hortons Cool to Killer's Endorsement." *National Post*, July 5, 2005, p. A1.

3. Thompson, M. "Re-examining 'Don't Ask, Don't Tell.'" http://www.time.com/time/nation/article/0,8599,1598653,00.html. Mar. 2007.

4. Karl, J. "Republican Rebukes Pace, but Defense Secretary Defends 'Don't Ask' Policy." http://abcnews.go.com/Politics/story?id=2947353&page=1. Mar. 2007.

5. Jefferson, T. http://www.brainyquote.com/quotes/quotes/t/thomasjeff101434.html. 2010.

Acknowledgments

A great many people are responsible for helping prepare this book. My coauthor Jeff Leeson brought clarity and structure to the project and I am grateful for his talent and involvement. Jossey-Bass editor Kathe Sweeney was supportive from the start, as were Natasha Nicholson and Heather Turbeville of the International Association of Business Communicators (IABC).

I thank my cousin Jeffrey Chernoff for lighting the initial spark that triggered my fascination with the world of news. As youngsters, Jeffrey and I would pretend we were newscasters and record ourselves on his tape machine as we read the daily paper aloud. We still have a hearty laugh when we recall announcing one story from the front page of the *Montreal Star* about "ruptured belly cockpits."

My dear friend Renee Kaminski gave me tremendous encouragement along the way and is in fact responsible for me getting my foot in the door of a major radio station. When we were fifteen years old, Renee and I would stand outside the local rock station hoping to meet disc jockeys, and one day, Earl Jive, a popular deejay, walked out the front door. "Show him your radio voice, Jeffrey, show him your radio voice," Renee said to me. So I did. Earl took a liking to me and let me volunteer at the station every afternoon after school, emptying ashtrays and taping ripped album jackets. Thank you, Earl.

I am eternally grateful to the late Casimir Stancyzkowski, who owned CFMB Radio in Montreal. After dropping out of high school at age seventeen, I worked in a men's clothing factory and, every day on my lunch hour, I would call the owners of different radio stations begging for an audition. Mr. Stancyzkowski offered me an audition if I promised to stop calling him. This was the opportunity I had been hoping for. Though I was convinced I blew the audition, Mr. Stancyzkowski called me the next day to tell me I was hired as morning news announcer. I thank him for believing in me and helping me leave my life at the factory.

It was Bob Holiday, news director of CFTR Radio in Toronto, who taught me to be a news reporter. Bob was a surly and hardnosed boss, who would threaten me daily. "I'll kick your ass down Yonge Street," he would say if I ever screwed up reporting a story. My gratitude also goes out to radio colleagues Brian Thomas, Tim Laing, Ben Steinfeld, and to CITY TV founder Moses Znaimer.

My entry into the world of media training is thanks to former CBC broadcaster Yvonne Burgess, who invited me to play the role of probing reporter in a media training program. I never properly thanked Yvonne, but I hope she knows how appreciative I am to her for opening a whole new world to me. My teachers in the world of public relations include Brian Hemming, president of Hill and Knowlton Canada, who brought me onboard to create a communications training division for the company. I also thank Jan Waterous, who succeeded Brian as president.

I have learned much from clients of Jeff Ansell & Associates as well. They include Sheila Frame, Kirsten Evraire, Natasha Bond, and Geoff Sprang, each of whom provided insight into the fictional Biojax scenario presented in the book. My appreciation is also extended to Greg Pruett of PG&E Corporation, who invited me to provide counsel in the company's handling of the Erin Brockovich case. A number of public relations professionals played a helpful role in editing the book. They include Karen Mortfield, Roy Thomas, Judith John, Peter Mueller, David Bauer, Bob Pickard, and Jordan Berman. I am grateful to each of them. Bert Goldstein played a role in the review process and my associate Shoana Prasad provided her insight as well. Thanks also to office colleagues Michelle Walker and Ariella Heskin.

In my research for the book, lawyer Jim Golden, Professor Kurt Dirks, and communications adviser Nick Morgan were kind enough to share their unique perspectives and it is much appreciated. My gratitude goes out as well to communications professionals Karen Rugen and Gary Gerdemann, who took the time to critique and edit an earlier, unpublished book. Very special thanks go to Larry Susskind and Michael Wheeler, who are both responsible for an important turning point in my career. In 1995, Larry and Mike kindly invited me to help teach the MIT-Harvard program, Dealing with an Angry Public. Their support and tremendous encouragement opened a great many doors for me and I thank them for making that possible. I am also grateful to Mike for my annual invitation to Harvard Business School, where I meet with his MBA students in the course Negotiating Complex Deals & Disputes. My role in the course is to help students appreciate the impacts of values and emotion on the negotiation process.

Adam and Joshua, my sons, played a role as well. Adam helped edit the book, and Josh, who studied radio in college, provided research assistance. Finally, this book and in fact, my career as a communications adviser would not have been possible without the faith, love, and support of my wife Annie. When the world of media training initially presented itself, Annie encouraged me to take the chance and go for it. Through every step of our friendship and marriage, she has been by my side and I could not have asked for a more wonderful life partner. Thank you, Annie.

The Authors

Jeff Ansell

When Jeff Ansell used to walk into the newsroom every day, his editors would ask, "Well Jeff, whose life will you ruin today?" As an investigative journalist prior to his consulting career, Jeff captured Nazi war criminals and posed undercover as a drug addict to expose doctors pushing drugs. He received the Radio and Television News Directors Association Award for the Most Significant Contribution to the Improvement of News Gathering in the country and was nominated for Canada's Governor-General's Award for public service in journalism.

Jeff, who was an executive at PR firm Hill and Knowlton, later formed Jeff Ansell & Associates, where he counseled PG&E Corporation in the Erin Brockovich case and media-trained White House spokespeople. Jeff has been an associate of the program "Dealing with an Angry Public" at Harvard Law School and lectures MBA students annually on media skills at Harvard Business School. Jeff Ansell is based in Toronto, Canada, and can be contacted at jeff@jeffansell.com.

Jeffrey Leeson

Jeffrey Leeson is a professional writer and editor. He can be contacted at jeffleeson@yahoo.com.

Index